Dedication

To our children


SATYA, CERI
TRISHA, STEVE


who gave us this knowledge...

# ACKNOWLEDGEMENTS

We would like to thank all, persons and organisations, who kindly commented on an earlier draft of this book.

We wish to mention, in particular, Chris Eames-Jones, Greg Condry, Tina Bruce, Safder Alladina, Mary Fawcett, Pauline Walsh, Gulzar Kanji, Ama Gueye, and Annette Douglas. A special mention, too, for Judith Koetter whose contribution to this Project has been considerable.

Bronwen Cohen, of the Equal Opportunities Commission, and Hazel Pennell, of the Information Section of the ILEA Research and Statistics Branch, kindly gave us every assistance in our frequent requests for information. And Bala Thind, from Southwark Council for Community Relations, resourcefully arranged the translations of "Educating The Whole Child" into the languages shown on the cover, at very short notice indeed.

A special word of thanks to Amanda Saunders, our Administrative Assistant, who not only typed the manuscript but whose invaluable supportive role in many other ways, gave us the space and freedom to complete this book

# CONTENTS

# INTRODUCTION

Building Blocks was established by SCF in 1984 as an 'anti-racist project for the under-fives' at a time when, as an issue, anti-racism - or at least a host of initiatives aimed at combatting racial inequality across various sectors and institutions of British society - enjoyed a high profile in many inner city areas. In the main, this represented an institutional response to the undeniable facts of race inequality in contemporary Britain - racial harassment in schools and on estates, police brutality, deportations, hunt for 'illegal' immigrants, discriminations in employment, as well as in the provision of housing, health, and other services.

Of course, these conditions still exist. In our view, however, they merely represent *one* dimension of social inequality in contemporary Britain, and it is indeed the phenomenon of inequality that needs to be addressed as a whole rather than be broken down into separate 'causes' and tackled through single-issue, and very often mutually antagonistic, pressure-groups. In the real world, competition for funding and for other social resources invariably tends to be accompanied by ideological positions which seek to establish each lobby's right to the 'most deserving' status - hardly a recipe for solidarity and collective unity.

At the same time, the delegating of 'race' or 'gender' issues to separate sub-committees or specialist units allows mainstream institutions and agencies to continue to treat these issues as marginal to their 'real work', and to evade their ultimate responsibilities. In these conditions, it is hardly surprising that the prevailing modes of combatting social inequalities and discriminations, while attracting a great deal of, predictably negative, media attention, have failed to secure any structural improvement in the condition of various inner-city communities.

This small book proposes a 'holistic' approach at two different but inter-related levels: at the conceptual level of linking the diverse strands of social inequality and at the practical level of a positive approach to a curriculum for Early Years.

In its simplest form, this philosophy implies the belief that systems can only be properly understood when seen as a unified and inter-related whole rather than a sum of their separate parts. It sees the division of human experience into rigidly separated categories as inconsistent with the unity and spontaneity of life-experience and attributes this fragmentation of experience to social control, which enshrines and legitimizes some forms of knowledge and excludes others. It is also worth emphasizing that holism is a multi-cultural concept: a relatively recent discovery in the West, holistic philosophies have long been prominent in Indian, Chinese, and African civilizations (e.g. the Indian spring festival of Holi, the Chinese spiritual philosophy of Tao).

In relation to social inequality, holism implies the recognition of the relationships between its various factors (e.g. racism, class, gender) and an understanding of these relationships through the locating of their root historical causes; hence we have put more weight, in the initial chapters, on a historical rather than on a purely sociological, introduction to the curriculum. Historical interpretation can never of course be a wholly objective exercise and perceptions will vary depending on the historian's national, cultural, class, or gender allegiances. We have provided our particular perspective, which carries a measure of our own experiences and those of the communities we belong to.

We then go on to a brief survey of 'education' since educational theories and practices are always shaped by specific historical processes and must be understood in the context of the prevailing social, economic, and political climate of their epoch. Nowhere is this better illustrated than in our main area of interest, early years, where monocultural assumptions and practice faithfully reflects the way British society tends to see itself; and where lack of provision and the unwillingness to see this age-group as the first phase of the education system is intimately linked to prevailing patterns of women's subordination and their unequal access to the labour market. Even more disturbing, perhaps, are the questions that this situation raises about the valuing of children in contemporary British society.

In relation to young children, a holistic approach signifies valuing the 'whole' child, i.e. recognising the inter-relatedness of the child's emotional, social, spiritual, and cognitive qualities, while also being aware that the harmonious 'growth' of these qualities depends on valuing the child's 'sense of belonging' to a particular family and community; and it also implies recognition of the overall social and environmental conditions which affect how children, families, and communities live and learn.

We are acutely aware that only a positive curriculum philosophy (rather than an approach based on a negative principle) can enable all children to acquire the skills, knowledge, and social attributes appropriate for living in a multi-cultural society. The longest sections of this essay outline a curriculum model based on the dimensions of cultural identity, gender equality, diversity, and co-operation. Within this guiding philosophy, all children discover themselves while learning a range of life-skills and social abilities which, in our view, would enable them to achieve educationally and, as a result, to creatively influence the direction of a changing society. Of course, the organisational implications of such an approach are considerable: a 'whole school' approach, a high level of teacher motivation, collaborative teaching, a warm and inviting school atmosphere, a close school/home relationship are all essential conditions for the successful implementation of such a curriculum.

An essential feature of this philosophy is that whatever the field of interest or inquiry, a holistic perspective always involves going further and deeper. Our modest claim to originality lies in the fact that we have attempted to outline, probably for the first time, a holistic approach to early years education *in the context of present day British society.* But we must also point out that what we are presenting here are merely the first steps of what promises to be a long and exciting journey.

Part I
# THE CONTEXT

# Chapter 1
# HISTORY AND SOCIETY

In Britain, inequalities in living standards and in health have been widening in recent years (Child Poverty Action Group Report, 1987). In conurbations like Greater London, such inequalities are also widening, as between inner and outer areas (Townsend, 1987). Comparative statistics of local authority areas place Tower Hamlets and the adjoining borough of Hackney at the top of all the league tables on indices of social deprivation (e.g. poor housing, unemployment, racial harassment), and at the bottom of those for good health, educational achievement and economic prosperity (Smith, 1985). Also, areas in the North such as Manchester/Salford, and Northern Ireland, tend to experience forms of material deprivation more severe than areas in the South, including areas of Greater London (Townsend, 1988).

In 1988 SCF was one of the organisations which made representations to Tower Hamlets Council on behalf of Bengali families who had been refused council accommodation on the grounds that by coming from Bangladesh to join their families, they had 'voluntarily made themselves homeless'! In the recent past other charities and voluntary organisations have added their weight to demands from community groups, small businesses, trade unions, and women's organisations for urgent and imaginative action from both central and local government to regenerate the inner city, while environmental organisations have called for the 'greening' of cities - i.e. greater provision of parks, open spaces, city farms, action on pollution, more imaginative housing - to reverse the steady deterioration of the urban quality of life.

There are, of course, a number of contemporary factors which account for the widening social inequalities in Britain. The abandonment of full employment policies dates back from 1967, leading to a situation of mass unemployment; moreover, social welfare state expenditure has been relatively smaller in Britain than in most other OECD countries over the past twenty-five years, and the effects of this situation have been further aggravated by recent cuts in both the scope and value of social security benefits. Income tax policies have also become less progressive, while the 1970s and early 1980s witnessed an unprecedented high rate of closure of manufacturing firms as well as other forms of withdrawal of investment from inner city areas (e.g. decline in urban aid programmes and in the real value of rate support grants). Finally, the British economy is itself being restructured by powerful multinational companies which are less accountable to the nation/state than were family firms and national companies in the early decades after the second world war (Townsend, 1988).

In essence, however, present-day social inequalities have historical rather than contemporary origins. Concern about 'the inner city', for instance, dates back to the industrial revolution which created the 'city slums' inhabited by the urban poor. And Stedman Jones has pointed out the existence of an 'outcast London' in the second half of the nineteenth century, essentially made up of an 'underclass' of casual labourers whose presence in the East End was seen as a serious threat to the very fabric of Victorian civilization and Conservative social order (Stedman Jones, 1971). A brief historical survey of some of the events that have contributed to the present conditions is therefore necessary.

Contemporary Britain is a multi-cultural, multi-racial, multi-lingual and multi-faith society. However, there exist political, social and economic contradictions in British society between the diversity of its peoples and cultures and the extent to which this is reflected in its social institutions and its core cultural values as well as in the unequal access to economic and material well-being. Defined as racism, this situation owes its origins and subsequent development to four centuries of British imperial and economic domination of large parts of the Southern World - Africa, India, the Caribbean, China, as well as parts of South-East Asia and the Middle East, that created both the material conditions and cultural perceptions which, in the form of racist ideologies, allowed the British, and particularly the English, to see the colonized peoples as 'inferior'.

It is however important to emphasise that Britain's overseas imperial expansion and conquests were pre-dated by England's conquest and subjugation of the Celtic nations of Britain - Wales, Ireland and Scotland. As one historian has put it, with reference to Britain, 'nation-building in its earliest stages might better be thought of as empire-building' (Hechter, 1975).

In this context, the annexation of Wales (1536), and the Acts of 'Union' with Scotland and Ireland (1707 and 1801 respectively) are events that are as significant to the history of English colonialism as the birth of the English Slave Trade (1552) when John Hawkins first transported enslaved Africans to the Caribbean, the battle of Plassey (1757) which effectively established British rule in India, or the Opium Wars (1839-1842) which 'opened up' China to British imports of Opium.

The 'anglicization' of the Celtic periphery through the promotion of English values, language, and religion rested on the firm belief that Norman Anglo-Saxon culture was inherently superior to Celtic culture.  Resistance to English 'internal colonialism' reached a peak in the early part of this century with the creation of the Irish Free State (Republic of Ireland), just as cumulative resistance to British rule later led to many colonies (e.g. India, Kenya) gaining national independance. It was also in the first decades of this century that women's growing demands for equal rights and opportunities found expression in the successful Suffragettes Campaign for votes for women.

Unification and pacification of Britain by an English ruling class also meant the establishment of a national administration and the disappearance of internal barriers to the circulation of goods and people - indispensable conditions for the development of industrial capitalism.  The 'industrial revolution' was also made possible by the enormous profits from the slave trade;  by the destruction of Indian industry and the importing of raw cotton from Bengal;  and by the massive employment of Irish labour in English factories.

The process of industrialization also led to the birth of the wage-earning urban working-class whose harsh living and working conditions were vividly documented by leading contemporary observers such as Dickens and Engels. It was also expected to diminish, and eventually to eradicate, regional cultural identities. However, the continued existence of Irish, Welsh, and Scottish nationalist movements testifies to the incomplete success of the English in assimilating, on their terms, indigeneous national minorities within the concept of 'Britishness'.

Many thinkers have also seen the industrial revolution as unleashing the modern technological forms of exploitation of natural resources and control over the environment which, motivated by the profits of unlimited production (and unlimited consumption!), has led to the gradual erosion of renewable resources and threatens a world-wide ecological disaster (Capra, 1982).

After the second world war, acute labour shortages in the manufacturing and services industries meant that Britain was able to use its colonies as a source of cheap labour. The period 1945-1975 saw the settlement in Britain of communities originating from the Caribbean, the Indian sub-continent, South-East Asia, Eastern and Southern Europe. Most of these communities initially arrived as invited migrant labour though some groups, e.g. Poles, Indians from East Africa, Chileans, and Vietnamese also came as political refugees.

These brief, and essentially suggestive historical observations simply serve to illustrate the complex web of historical relationships which have contributed to the creation of the present range of inequalities in contemporary British society. Britain is not simply a multi-cultural society characterized by diversity: this diversity is itself embodied in subordinate social groups who face a range of inequalities and discriminations based on class, culture, race, gender, nationality, region. And inequality is the common condition which defines these otherwise very diverse social groups - industrial workers, unemployed Northerners, South Asians, Blacks, Irish, Welsh, Women, Travellers etc - in fact a vast majority of the population.

In effect, this means that while it is possible to speak of 'majority' and 'minorities' in terms of, say, race or language we do not believe that the notion of a 'white majority' is in any way *politically meaningful* as it in fact obscures rather than clarifies the diffuse patterns of inequality and subordination in present-day Britain.

It is far more meaningful to identify the dominance, or 'hegemony' of a minority class within the 'majority race' than the majority race per se, for this enables us to locate the *source* of political and economic predominance rather than simply identifying their effects. The essential character of the British ruling class has in fact remained remarkably constant since the days of Empire: Southern English, male, monolingual, monolithic, propertied, and bureaucratic.

Since 'White' cannot be seen as a meaningful political concept, the claims of 'Black' as a political category rest on even shakier foundations. A full critique of this notion has been made elsewhere (Hazareesingh, 1986) and it is here only possible to summarize the arguments. this definition of 'Black'

- rests on 'taking on' a simplistic and negative 'black-and-white' dualism characteristic of racist thinking;

- by focusing on 'White' people as an undifferentiated negative mass, it denies the reality of class as the main instrument of political domination and the basic source of social inequalities;

- unlike other political concepts (e.g. socialism, feminism, ecology) it lacks any positive philosophy, offers no vision of an 'alternative society', and does not imply any programmatic content;

- defines groups of people purely through their negative experiences in a *particular* society, and as a result, it

- denies the positive, cultural focus of 'Black' as a source of collective pride established by people of African descent throughout the world, which remains the term's primary significance; and also

- denies other groups (e.g. people of Indian descent) the strength of their positive, historically-created identities indispensable to the struggle against racism and other inequalities, and obscures perceptions ofsolidarity with their own people in other parts of the world;

- engenders a great deal of confusion all round (e.g. "I'm not sure what to call you" or "applications from black people are welcomed") and in effect works against people coming together on a genuine political basis.

Building Blocks uses definitions based on positive cultural concepts rather than on how communities might be abstractly and problematical viewed by the British state. Hence 'Black' is used to refer solely to peoples of African descent, i.e. African and African-Caribbean communities; the term 'Asian' is only used as a collective description of all communities originating from the (massive!) continent of Asia (e.g. Indian, Chinese, Vietnamese, etc.). Communities originating from the narrower area of the Indian sub-continent are referred to, in geographical terms, as 'South Asian', and in cultural terms, as 'Indian'.

We do, of course, recognise the numerous national/regional/ religious variations within both 'South Asian' and 'Black', and are aware, too, that people often hold strong regional identities especially when a particular region also displays a distinctive language and culture (e.g. Bengal, Gujarat, Panjab). Acknowledging such identities is of course particularly important when working with young children.

Nonetheless, we also feel that 'core' cultural definitions (e.g. Indian) are suggestive of a shared 'civilizational' history amongst many communities settled in Britain who, in the southern world today, often find themselves artificially separated by national boundaries which are the product not of choice, but of British imperial policies.

# Chapter 2
# EDUCATION

In a multi-cultural society characterized by a variety of social inequalities, the functions of 'education' and of the educator need to be reassessed. Historically, mainstream education relied heavily on teacher-centred instruction and stressed the virtues of formal English literacy, monolingualism*, individualism, competitiveness, and abstractness, which are of course both class-specific and culture-specific values (Reynolds and Skilbeck, 1976). Indeed, the experience of education was held to be 'beneficial' precisely to the extent that it was at odds with the everyday life and common experiences of most children.

Education curricula never made explicit their cultural biases and assumptions, and this allowed educators to believe that they were adopting 'culture-blind' approaches and passing on 'value-free' knowledge. This absence of cultural self-consciousness itself reflected 'English' hegemony and its success in establishing minority class values as national, and indeed universal ones. In this sense curricula were essentially variations on a selection from the dominant culture of British society, concerned to transmit established values, skills and knowledge from the privileged of one generation to the privileged of the next, and faithfully reproducing existing social inequalities in the process.

*No longer perhaps the undisguised blessing it once was. A recent European Commission survey shows Britons to be the worst linguists in Europe with every prospect of missing out on the many benefits arising from the removal of Common Market trade barriers in 1992. The survey reveals that 70% of young Britons aged between 15 and 24 cannot hold a simple conversation in a foreign language. In contrast in Luxembourg, 53% of young people in the same age group can hold a conversation in *three* languages (*Times Educational Supplement*, 25.11.'88).

This unquestioned monocultural nature of the curriculum more than nullified the intended effects of 'progressive' educational legislation such as the 1944 Education Act which sought to establish the principle of equality of opportunity. The historic failure of British education to meet the needs and fulfil the potential of children from working-class backgrounds (Keddie, 1971) has more recently been matched by a similar inability to provide meaningful and motivating learning experiences for children from the new communities of Britain, with similar results (DES 1981; 1985); while research carried out in the 1970s established considerable gender inequalities both in the provision of educational opportunities and in attainment (Delamont, 1980; DES 1982).

In the early childhood tradition, this 'transmission' model of education is still evident in notions of the child as a (largely passive) 'recipient' of knowledge and as an individualised 'adult-in-the-making'. This leads to a prescriptive view of the curriculum in which the adult's role is to search out the missing skills, select appropriate learning experiences and transmit them to the child. Children are seen as needing to be moulded into the kind of shape necessary for them to 'fit in' society and its prevailing norms. And this appears to be the view of the child implicit in Mr Baker's *National Curriculum*.

This concept of the child as an 'unfinished' adult shifts the focus away from the child's own intentions, attachments, and strivings - which might in fact open up many learning horizons for the *adult*, on to an end-product notion of adulthood which is unwisely equated with 'achieved knowledge'. It might be said that this represents a specifically western, 'rationalist' approach to both childhood and learning which by separating the mind from the heart, effectively denies the essential unity of the child.

In Indian, Chinese, and African cultures, on the other hand, childhood was never seen primarily as a transitory stage of individualistic development towards adulthood, but as a fully meaningful world-in-itself with its own way of being, seeing, and feeling. Indian philosophies, for instance, stress that the child should not simply be 'brought up': there is an accompanying responsibility for the adult to enter into the child's mode of experiencing the world (Kakar, 1981).

This conception of childhood as a meaningful world-in-itself, which is common to many cultures of the southern world, is rooted in a very distinctive philosophical perception of humankind's place in the world. This tradition stresses the unity and inter-dependency of all living elements with their natural environment, and sees human existence in collective rather than individualistic terms, emphasizing co-operation rather than competition. As a result, the concept of the 'individual child', as separate from family and community does not exist. Something of this holistic spirit pervades the writings of the German educationist Froebel whose "notion of 'kindergarten', the garden of children, partly emphasises nature, partly community, and partly family" (Bruce, 1987, p.13).

The quality of education in the early years, however is only partly dependent on the philosophical assumptions and theoretical arguments by which it is informed: it is also dependent on the institutional arrangements that allow early years provisions to exist in the first place and on the 'quality' of both the human and the material resources that are allocated to them. These, in turn, are very much governed by prevailing political and societal views and priorities in relation to children, families and education.

The division of the initial phase of Early Years into 'care' and 'education' common to Britain and to other EEC countries, is accompanied by inequalities in staff qualifications, status, skills, and parental expectations, which go back to the class origins of this division in the aftermath of the industrial revolution (Cohen, 1988). Another factor is the endemic shortage of nursery/primary teachers from the new communities of Britain, partly caused by the DES's refusal to recognise teaching qualifications from Asia, Africa, the Caribbean, Southern Europe, and Latin America. And the decline, over the past ten years, of *real* state investment in education as well as increased centralized control over the teaching process has led to a steady deterioration in teachers' working conditions (e.g. unacceptably high teacher-children ratios). This situation means that many children's early learning takes place in less than satisfactory conditions, especially in inner-city areas.

In Britain only one local authority, Strathclyde has integrated all services for under-fives within the education department; in contrast a proposed new Education Act would make Spain the first EEC state to establish the 0-6 age group as the initial stage of the education system, making education authorities responsible for all childcare services (Moss, 1988, p.124). It is in terms of public provision for young children, however, that the gap between Britain and other EEC member-states is most significant, and even Portugal, nominally at the bottom of the table (Table 1) still spends, in relation to its GNP, proportionately more on childcare than Britain (Ibid).

Moreover, there is also considerable regional disparity in provision within Britain. Northern Ireland, for instance, has little nursery education provision, the lowest proportion of playgroup places, and admits a high proportion of three and four year olds straight into primary school. In contrast, the London Borough of Hounslow offers places in nursery education for more than eight out of ten three and four year olds (compared to a national average of just under four out of ten), whereas fourteen of the non-metropolitan counties in England have places for less than 10% of this age group, and Gloucestershire has no places at all (Cohen, 1988, p.126).

Cohen attributes this situation to the re-emergence of the traditionalist view of women's role in society (that 'woman's place is in the home'), and points to the widening income gap between men and women over the past ten years caused by an erosion of women's employment opportunities. It may also be the case, in addition, that an awareness of the beneficial effects of early education, as shown by a recent Child Health and Education Study Report which found that children from all social classes and ethnic groups benefitted from attending a

## TABLE 1

### Public provision for 3-5 year olds in Member States of the European Community

| Country | Proportion of 3-5's | Full-time | Hours Available |
|---|---|---|---|
| FRANCE | 95%+ | All | 8 |
| BELGIUM | 95%+ | All | 5-6 |
| ITALY | 88% | 66% | 7 |
| DENMARK | 87% | 60% | 7 |
| SPAIN | 66% | All | 7 |
| GREECE | 62% | 17% | 7 |
| WEST GERMANY | 60% | 12% | 8 |
| IRELAND | 52% | None | 4 |
| NETHERLANDS | 50% | All | 5-7 |
| LUXEMBURG | 48% | 24% | 6 |
| UNITED KINGDOM | 44% | 19% | 6 |
| PORTUGAL | 25% | All | 7 |

Source: *Childcare and Equality of Opportunity: Consolidated Report to the European Commission, Peter Moss EEC Childcare Network April 1988.*

pre-school education facility (Osborn and Milbank, 1988), continues to be low amongst local and central education decision-makers as well as in society generally.

The last decade has seen an increase in the number of children experiencing nursery education, consistent with parents' growing preference for this type of provision (Table 2). This has mainly come about, however, as a result of a shift from full-time to part-time provision rather than an increase in the number of nursery classes and schools (Cohen, op. cit. p.45). The expansion of part-time, at the cost of full-time, nursery education is probably compatible with the recommendations of the 1967 Plowden Report, although the complete failure to reach even the modest targets set by the 1972 DES White Paper (of part-time education for 50% of 3 year olds and 90% of 4 year olds by 1980) makes it far more likely to be a 'rationing' device reflecting the continued low priority of early years education in Official thinking.

The Plowden Report has also generally been seen as confirming some progressive approaches to educating young children such as 'child-centredness', active learning through play, flexible teaching methods and informal classroom organisation, derived from an earlier era of progressive pioneers such as Froebel and the McMillan sisters. Indeed, the 'good practice classroom' has been defined as one "where all the children are actively engaged in exploration and discovery, and where the teacher moves around consulting, guiding and stimulating individual children or occasionally, where convenient, groups of children who are at similar developmental stages. She or he has intimate knowledge of the physical, intellectual, and social level of each child and knows, therefore, when and how best to stimulate and intervene with each one" (Chazan et. al., 1987, p.21).

The term 'child-centredness' frequently arouses controversy and it is true that there are 'laissez-faire' interpretations of the concept which perceive the child's development as "laid down by intrinsic patterning prior to and independent of actual experience" (Bruce, op. cit. p.4) and are therefore concerned to

TABLE 2

Parents' preferred type of provision, 1974, 1983 and 1985

|  | 1974<br>(PPA)<br>Base: 2501<br>% | 1983<br>(PPA)<br>367<br>% | 1985<br>(PPA)<br>400<br>% |
|---|---|---|---|
| LA Nursery School/Class | 20 | 42 | 42 |
| LA Day Nursery | 7 | 10 | 11 |
| Private Nursery | NA | 6 | 10 |
| Playgroup | 25 | 39 | 38 |
| Creche | 1 | 2 | 3 |
| Mother-and-toddler Group | NA | 12 | 14 |
| Childminder | 3 | 4 | 3 |
| None | 37 | 10 | 10 |

Source: *Caring for Children: Services and Policies for Childcare and Equal Opportunities in the United Kingdom – Report for the European Commission's Childcare Network, Bronwen Cohen, 1988.*

minimize the role of the adult since "if we only learn to let live, the plan for growth is all there" (Ibid p.5). This perspective tends to see the child in purely individualistic terms as the sole instigator of his/her knowledge, and in isolation from his/her social and cultural context. However, most advocates of 'child-centredness' would argue that the child can only genuinely be 'centred on' through knowledge of his/her environmental context so that the curriculum becomes "the meeting ground where children and teachers share intentions" (Blenkin and Kelly, 1988, p.76).

It seems to us that the real difficulty with child-centredness, is that it has never been explicitly defined in relation to Britain as a multi-cultural and class-divided society. A child-centred approach emphasizes the fact that meaningful learning can only occur if what the child brings in terms of concrete experiences is seen by the teacher as the essential component in his/her planning of the curriculum and in the (resource-based) organization of the classroom environment.

However, 'concrete experiences' may still be interpreted according to both monocultural and middle-class teacher assumptions which means that in practice many children's cultural and social experiences may continue to be silenced within the curriculum. Indeed, teachers and carers may often select materials and activities which they have, over the years, come to value themselves and assume that they represent what is familiar to and valued by all children: their speech, gestures, intonation, body language, their selection of play materials, books, and learning resources, the aspects of the world outside which they choose to represent in the classroom or playroom, all communicate values and attitudes which may not only be unfamiliar to many children but may also seem to reject their own experiences.

In our view, it is these absences, these silences which damage the child's shared sense of cultural and social identity with his/her family and community, that lie at the heart of the social oppressions and inequalities of racism and class as they operate in early years:

- *racism* essentially operates through the silencing and invisibility of the child's cultural and racial identity in the learning environment through both the play and learning materials that are provided and the teacher/carer's ethos, style of communication, and values; the silencing of the child's home language, the invisibility his/her history, the absence of familiar food, music and clothes, the non or negative references to skin-colour, features, family and spiritual values.

- *class* inequality is, similarly, reinforced through play and learning materials that render the child's home values and social experience invisible, and by the teacher/carer's negative assessment of working-class parents and occupations; by the absence of working-class role-models, in books or 'play-people' the invisibility of its history, the non-acceptance of the child's class or regional dialect.

- *gender* discrimination is, on the other hand, maintained and reinforced by the actual emphasis on, and highlighting of, socially constructed gender differences. Discrimination operates, once again, through books and play materials which generally offer girls a far more restricted range of roles than boys, roles that are moreover mainly passive and home-centred in contrast to the action-oriented, energetic, exploratory and leadership roles offered to boys to identify with; also through teachers/carers acquiescence in gender-stereotyped play activities and situations and in their use of gender as an organizing principle and management strategy within their classrooms.

Such absences and silences, discriminations and negative attitudes indicate the need to re-assess the concept of child-centredness in the present condition of British society. Child-centredness, in our view, needs to be conceived in *holistic* terms which in this context, is defined by a range of inter-related dimensions.

A holistic philosophy of education implies opportunities for creative learning that are meaningful from the child's point of view, that are drawn from a diversity of cultural experiences, that maintain the unity of affective and cognitive dispositions, and that nurture an awareness of the importance of diverse life-sustaining processes in relation both to people and the natural environment. It is also process-oriented and sees learning very much in 'developmental' terms in relation, not to objectively-devised curriculum aims, but to the child's growing control over the processes of his/her knowledge acquisition.

This view does *not* see the child as the sole creator of his/her learning but considers the human environment of both adults and children, with whom the child interacts, as being of crucial importance. "There is interaction with what is external, but there is also interaction within the child" (Bruce, op. cit. p.6). In other words, both the child and the world he/she perceives are perpetually changing, exerting a continual modifying influence on each other.

As we shall see in later chapters the adult's role, in these interactions, is crucial. Perhaps the most significant initial factor, in our view, is an awareness of the social and cultural realities in which children live, in present-day Britain. A child's sense of cultural belonging provides him/her with a basic framework for understanding the world, but the complete details of his/her experience also depend on other 'locations' in society. Children have different experiences and put different meanings upon things depending on where they are, not only in terms of culture or race, but also in terms of class, gender, community, and geography (i.e. physical living environment). To give just one example, in Greater London 29% of children between the ages of two and nine live in flats, very often above the second floor, whereas in Wales only 1% live in similar circumstances (Mays, 1985, p.12).

These 'meanings' themselves change not only as family circumstances and locations change but also as children develop their own identities, establish peer relationships, widen their experiences, and construct their own interpretations.

No genuine child-centred curriculum can therefore be based on cultural or social assumptions *about* young children and their families; teachers and carers require concrete knowledge and information about each child's background and experiences as the indispensable means of motivating and extending their learning. This implies greater communication and closer collaboration between teachers, carers, and parents. It also means that teachers and carers require the essential qualities of openness, sensitivity and imagination in discovering and selecting those experiences that have most relevance in terms of the curriculum. Other enabling characteristics are high expectations of all children, accurate perceptions of children and parents, flexibility, warmth, and a capacity to motivate - and, of course, a committment to the view that the cultures children bring to school are worth preserving and enriching.

Part II
# THE CURRICULUM

# Chapter 3
# THE DEVELOPING CHILD

During the past decade the traditional view of child development in terms of 'ages and stages' has been increasingly called into question and the emphasis has shifted from 'when' to 'how' and 'why' a child learns.

In the words of two educationists, a "developmental approach to change must feature more than a chronological catalogue of differences tied to age. To say that a child holds a pen at ten months, first scribbles with interest at a year and a half, and draws representationally by four only mimics a developmental perspective. Only when one begins to focus on such issues as the rate at which this growth occurs, the steps by which the various landmarks are achieved, the organisation of physical, cognitive and social skills into a co-ordinated system for creating forms and infusing them with meaning, only then has one 'thought developmentally'" (Wolf and Gardner in Hauseman, 1980, p.51).

This shift has been accompanied by a concentration on what the child *can* do as opposed to what he/she cannot do. Studies have revealed that babies are born with a surprisingly rich and well-organised perceptual system, enabling them to make very early sense of their perceptions of people and things. By two weeks of age, for example, the child can identify his/her mother's voice and face. Babies also have an amazing ability to perceive distance, size, and direction and to recognize how senses relate - that what can be heard can perhaps be seen, and what seen perhaps touched (Bower, 1977). There is also evidence that, certainly by the end of their first year, children are already social beings, since they not only participate in, but also shape and direct, the pre-verbal interactions they have with others (Bruner, 1981).

Margaret Donaldson has seriously undermined Piaget's view of the young child as a purely 'egocentric' being until the age of five (i.e. as self-centred and unable to 'see' another's point of view), and has shown that when tasks require children as young as three to act in ways which are consistent with basic

29

human purposes and interactions, and which make 'sense' to them, they are well capable of 'decentring' (Donaldson, 1978, p.24).    She also rejects Piaget's limited view of the young child's cognitive abilities and argues that by the age of four children are quite able to reason deductively, as shown, for example, in the comments they make while listening to stories (Ibid, p.59).

Donaldson also takes issue with Chomsky's theory that children have an "innate acquisition device" which is specific to language, with the result that language is acquired faster than the other skills of the mind.    She maintains that children's language-learning faculties are inter-woven with the rest of their mental growth and that they are able to pick up language at such speed precisely because they have a well-developed capacity for making sense of situations involving direct and immediate human interaction (Ibid, pp.36-37).

Current thinking on learning in early years tends to suggest, therefore, that the child is, from birth, striving to make sense of his/her environment and to exercise some kind of self-directed control over it.    Play is the characteristic medium through which babies and infants try out a range of actions which express their search for meaning and consistency in their surroundings.    Once again, however, the quality of social interaction with adults in their environment is of crucial importance.

Barbara Tizard and Martin Hughes analysed tape-recordings of four year olds from both working and middle-class backgrounds in conversation with their mothers at home, and for comparison, with their teachers at school.    They found that at home the children talked freely about a wide range of topics: they initiated and sustained conversations, argued, and endlessly asked questions.    These conversations revealed the children as persistent and logical thinkers, striving to grasp new ideas.    The home thus provided a powerful learning environment.    The children's talk with teachers lacked such richness, depth and variety.    Nor was there the sense of intellectual struggle and mutual attempt to communicate found at home (Tizard and Hughes, 1984).

The main reasons suggested for this were:

- The extensive range of activities that took place within, or from the base of, the home

- The sharing of a common life between parent and child, stretching back into the past, and forward into the future

- The small number of children who shared the adult's time and attention

- Learning was embedded in contexts of great meaning to the child

- The close, often intense, relationship between mother and child

(Ibid. pp.250-251)

Earlier research by Wells (Wells, 1982) reaches similar conclusions. Although Tizard and Hughes are careful to point out that not all family settings (of course) offer rich learning environments, the home's potential advantages in this respect arise from the fact that it is a scene of 'real-life' situations in which "children have purposes and intentions and in which they can recognize and respond to similar purposes and intentions in others" (Donaldson, op. cit. p.121). The knowledge of homes and communities comes in a multiplicity of languages and dialects which express children's inner worlds of feelings, thoughts, and imagination. By the time they are introduced to a mainstream educational provision between the ages of 3 and 5, most children are, on their own terms, skilled thinkers and talkers.

# Chapter 4
# KNOWLEDGE OF THE CHILD

How can teachers and carers gain knowledge of children's initial skills, interests, and attachments which they bring from their homes and communities since, from a child-centred perspective, these constitute the first reference point in the process of curriculum planning?

In this respect, the crucial period for both the child and the teacher is the gradual process through which the child is received into his/her new environment, initially around the age of three (playground, nursery), and then at five (infant, primary). While it is clearly important for the teacher to identify children's initial interests and skills through interaction and observation during their first couple of weeks in the provision, awareness of their previous experience is essential to 'complete the picture'.

Such information-gathering clearly requires meaningful interaction between teachers/carers, parents, and children. Although communication is established at the time of the parents initial visit to the provision, and subsequently through teacher/carer home visits, more informal and potentially meaningful interaction can occur where e.g. parents and toddler groups, nurseries and primary schools are in close proximity. In this respect, there already are some examples of potential good practice, e.g. some ILEA provisions which combine parents and toddler group, nursery classes, and primary school all on one site, and where nursery staff periodically join the parents and toddler group.

This kind of structure, with its potential for a 'whole school' approach, may also enable nursery children to see themselves as part of an increasingly familiar community as well as promote regular communication between nursery and primary teachers, more effective teamwork, including collaborative teaching, and a strong measure of continuity in children's learning experiences. In these situations regular visits by the nursery children to the primary building (e.g. for assembly) as well as occasional visits by reception class teachers to the nursery, e.g. to introduce an activity or a story could help children build up confidence for the next stage of learning.

Essentially, however, the process of knowing the child can best be enhanced through teachers and parents engaging in an equal partnership in which both learn from each other: Teachers welcome parents' skills into the classroom while parents share in their children's school learning and follow it up at home. Since early learning is rooted in home experiences, teachers "must try to get this vast body of influences on to the school's side, or else face the possibility of having to start relating to the child, particularly the very young child, at a level of communication and cognitive activity much lower than that which the child confidently employs at home" (Hurst, 1988 pp.101-102). Parental involvement is particularly crucial during children's first experience of educational provision, providing them with reassuring elements of continuity while adjusting to their new environment. In this way, it also becomes possible for teachers and carers to build up, in collaboration with children and parents, individual child profiles which might help them establish each child's 'significant experiences' prior to arrival.

A 'child profile' might include:

- personal name: pronounciation, meaning

- cultural origin

- faith

- first language of child

- first language of parents

- language(s) spoken at home

- position in family

- play experiences

- experiences of stories

- travel experiences

- likes and dislikes

- parents' skills and interests

- pre-admission care (e.g. parents), other family, other adult(s), other provision, childminder)

- dietary special needs

- health

'Knowing the child', however, is an on-going process. The profile mainly serves as an initial source of reference enabling teachers and carers to organise provision and plan activities in a way that would relate to and build on the child's previous learning. The focus then rapidly switches to the processes of observation and interaction with children as well as regular, education-related communication with parents which might ensure that each child's continuing significant experiences maintain their relevance in terms of the teacher's planning of the curriculum.

# Chapter 5
# A HOLISTIC MODEL

In Early Years, learning is essentially unitary and 'holistic', i.e. the child combines and unifies various senses and skills in his/her interactions with both the human environment and play resources as well as with his/her 'inner' knowledge; as a result of these interactions, senses, skills, and knowledge are further enhanced. Educational objectives for the first seven years of a child's life (and beyond!) are primarily developmental, and there is considerable variation both in the speed at which individual children 'develop' skills and knowledge and in the levels of acquisition of the range of abilities, even by the age of seven.

Indeed, part of the excitement and challenge of working with this age-group lies in the fact that for young children, everything is in process, in a state of becoming: nothing is as yet fixed, definite, set. Identities are being developed and challenged, personal friendships are being establised and changed, skills are being learnt and forgotten, values - often contradictory ones - are being nurtured, talents are being discovered.

Much of recent educational thinking on Early Years stresses the necessity of a well-planned curriculum (Curtis, 1986; Bruce, 1987; Blenkin and Kelly, 1988) which would express the rich complexity of child development in these crucial years. A curriculum, in its broadest sense, can be defined as

> *the sum total of experiences that the child discovers within the learning environment, including both the planned activities and what has been called the "hidden curriculum", i.e., the quality of the play environment, attitudes towards children and towards parents,teacher / carer styles, values and expectations, relationships between children.*

It is also clear that over the 3-7 period a series of curricula would need to be devised at growing levels of complexity consistent with children's own growth in abilities, self-knowledge, social awareness, and learning autonomy.

Figure 1 presents an *initial* curriculum model.

This model is essentially dynamic and interactive: the categories of skills and aptitudes are 'broken up' for identification but then re-united at the centre, indicating both their common source - the child - and their interconnectedness. These inter-related developmental categories are also pervaded, or informed by the four principles of our philosophy - cultural identity, gender equality, diversity, and co-operation. All aspects of the model would be constantly interacting, so that everything pervades everything else.

Skills can, of course, be classified in a variety of ways, and Figure 1 merely suggests *one* method. Each category opens up a literally endless flow of relationships with the others. Viewed imaginatively (rather than in compartmentalized thinking terms), 'communication', for instance, involves communication with others (social) through talk (language), but also through body language, facial expression, gesture (physical), as well as through dance and drama (aesthetical); it also implies communication with self through developing a sense of awe, wonder and celebration (emotional/spiritual) and through reflecting on one's actions (cognitive). Again, the child's growing awareness of the many dimensions and multiple forms of beauty depends on an 'inter-disciplinary' exercising of senses and skills. Nor are there any 'purely physical' activities. Cognitive, physical, and emotional growth develop alongside one another, each contributing to the other; while viewed, as process, language is about sounds, talk, thought, symbolic representation, and literacy.
The four philosophical elements are defined as follows:

- *Cultural identity* incorporates, within the framework of culture, both the 'race' dimension of the child's identity and his/her 'class' experience. It is defined as 'whatever a child holds to be emotionally meaningful and significant both about himself/herself and in his/her life', e.g. skin colour, features, mother-tongue, food, dress, music/songs, heritage myths and legends, culturally specific home objects, family relationships and occupations.

FIGURE 1

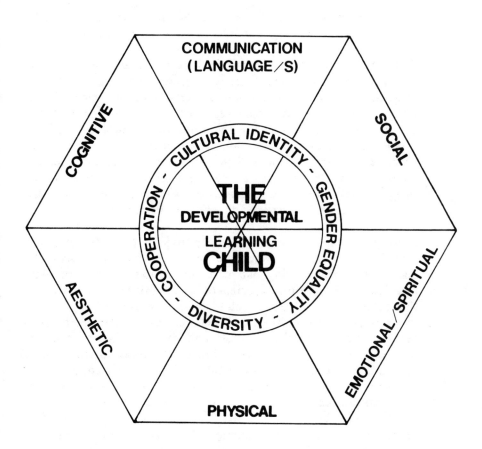

- *Gender equality* is defined as 'the breaking down of socially restrictive gender roles through offering both boys and girls equally, active and exploring as well as tender and nurturing roles'.

- *Diversity* is 'the different cultural and environmental realities both in society and in the world'.

- *Co-operation* signifies both 'children learning together' and 'children learning from, and about each other'.

The three elements of the curriculum model are therefore the child, knowledge, and a guiding philosophy. The fourth, 'hidden' dimension is the child's environment, made up of people, places and play resources. Within this environment it is teachers and carers who link the child and knowledge, and activate the guiding philosophy, thus turning the model into practice. From the teacher's point of view, therefore, the curriculum can be defined as the provision of the most appropriate learning experiences to encourage optimum development of a range of creative life-skills in each child.

It follows from the model that curricula for the 3-7 age group would be negotiated, interactive processes. In other words, the actual, detailed working out of a curriculum in terms of play activities and learning experiences would take into account (a) the cultural variety of the children in the provision; (b) the diversity, in both cultural and class terms, of the speech patterns of children; (c) the skills and experiences of *each individual child*; (d) the composition of the local community; (e) the nature of the local environment. It is in this context that information from the child profiles might provide a most useful starting point.

Since the purpose of the curriculum is to maximize learning possibilities for all children while reinforcing each child's cultural identity as well as his/her social and spiritual awareness, the selection of themes or topics through which at least part of the curriculum will unfold might be based on (a) each topic's ability to relate to *all* the areas of the curriculum, (b) each topic's meaningfulness in terms of children's experiences and interests, (c) each topic's potential for motivating children's autonomous, further learning, (d) thematic inter-relationships.

Curriculum planning essentially involves the recognition of a longer temporal process, i.e. the organisation of the sequence of learning episodes: it may include flow charts of thematic work, open to constant revision and adjustment to allow for variations in individual children's pace of learning as well as to support changing directions in their interests, and the new learning possibilities these open up. Indeed, if the holistic approach is maintained, 'development' and 'curriculum' should synchronise.

A curriculum model which takes as its starting-point the child's life experiences as part of a family and community provides the two ingredients which are most likely to contribute to successful learning: previous experience and motivation (Curtis, 1986). The child will be developing skills and knowledge based upon his/her earlier experiences and will be more likely to see the relevance of provision-based activities if the ideas arise from his/her immediate environment. And since this process also involves communication with, and participation by parents in these early stages of their children's education, they will be more likely to both understand and support the provision's educational philosophy and practice.

# Chapter 6
# THE LEARNING ENVIRONMENT

A fundamental premise of good practice is the existence of adequate playspace where indoor and outdoor space combine to provide an integrated school learning environment which is warm, safe, clean, secure and aesthetically pleasing. Children's emotional well-being is further enhanced when at least some part of the indoor visual environment reflects their identities and experiences, e.g. culturally appropriate images and illustrations, familiar, home-related objects, names attractively written up in the range of languages represented in the provision.

The overall visual impact of the learning environment has a profound influence on both the children who work there and the parents who visit it. A recent report on design in education argues that planning the classroom involves elements of design which must be successfully accomplished if the play environment is to be inviting, stimulating and conducive to learning. The report adds that teachers should not only develop design skills themselves but should involve children in these processes as well, through e.g. exploring three-dimensional shapes, mounting exhibitions, making books, creating gardens, and building working models (Blenkin and Kelly, op. cit. p.49).

Adequate indoor playspace can be defined as an overall area large enough to be organised into smaller flexibly defined play areas, e.g. carpeted quiet areas (book-corner, home-corner, listening-corner), messy areas and spaces where children can freely manipulate, construct, and create (art and craft corner, small/large construction, sand and water, cooking, music corner), and finally, bays and corners where children can 'collaborate' and prolong a particular play activity; within each of these areas, moreover, children should be able to move freely and safely and have easy access to choosing and returning materials. This promotes learning autonomy and allows teachers and carers to engage in sustained interaction with other individual, or groups of, children.

Adequate outdoor playspace can be described as an overall area which allows children a wide variety of opportunities for both active physical experience and for learning about their natural environment (digging area, plants, garden). Once again, the outdoor area should be spacious enough for children to move around freely and, when appropriate, to 'get away' from adults.

The environment must therefore offer a framework for the development of skills, values, and understandings which should always be supported by children's present lived experience. Indeed, curriculum provision in early years is primarily about multi-cultural resource-based learning environments. Access to a rich range of resources, and experience of diverse symbolic forms enable children to formulate their own questions and pursue their own hypotheses, and hence to *discover knowledge for themselves*. The content of learning resources might therefore be based on the following factors:

- appropriateness in terms of the breadth of the curriculum

- appropriateness in terms of the children's progressive developmental enhancement during both 3-5 and 5-7 phases

- relatedness to the cultural identities of the children

- potential for stimulating co-operative play

- potential for fostering a positive self-image for all the children

- potential for stimulating children's sense of curiosity and motivation

- ability to positively reflect different peoples, cultures, places, and environments both in society and in the world

In common with most educationists, we would regard the following as basic:

- Story area: picture books, story-books, story tapes, props,

41

puppets, cut-outs, provision for making own stories...

- Home corner: dressing up clothes, a variety of household and domestic objects, dolls, soft toys, soft blocks...

- Music/listening corner: musical instruments, sound-making objects, taped music and stories, song books and rhymes...

- Literacy materials: stories, lined and plain paper, pads, notebooks, coloured papers, tracing paper, pens, pencils, crayons, telephones, typewriters, wooden/magnetic/block letters, alphabet friezes, collage materials, plasticine, news-papers, magazines, sellotape, sticky labels...

- Art and Craft: easels, paints, brushes, crayons, printing-blocks, collage, papers, scissors, fabrics, clay, dough, plasticine, lacing and sewing equipment, twigs, tree roots, pressed flowers, leaves, shells...

- Small world/small construction: A variety of Mecano, Lego, bricks, small wooden blocks, railway tracks, puzzles, miniature people, lottos, games...

- Large construction: large wooden blocks, covers, planks, ladders, tyres, plastic crates, tools...

- Early maths: stories, puzzles, posting box, shop telephones, bricks, construction toys, weighing and measuring equipment, egg boxes, number friezes, sets of objects, games, a range of materials of different sizes, games, maps, papers, writing equipment...

- Physical: climbing frame, see-saw, slide, tunnel, large wheeled toys, skipping ropes...

- Environmental/Science/Technology: sand, water, clay, pebbles, gravel, shells, conkers, digging area, plants, small gardening equipment; bricks weighing and measuring equipment, sets of objects, mechanical objects, magnifying glasses; cooker, cooking utensils, recipes, ingredients; natural and play materials of varied dimensions, textures, sounds, smells, and tastes...

- Reference materials: information books, newspapers, magazines, dictionaries, maps...

Once again, these resources have, from the outset, to be conceived in multi-cultural and multi-lingual terms. It is also important to bear in mind that although the learning environment can be, for organisational purposes, separated out in this way (and there could be other ways of classifying resources), it needs to be thought of as a *whole* unit. The enhancement of the child's developmental skills depends on his/her physical movements and interactions within the entire environment, and it would be wholly unproductive to equate the discovery or learning of particular skills with specific areas of the classroom.

For instance, cooking may be seen, in terms of its end-product, as a creative, even artistic activity. However, the *process* involves a range of movements (e.g. to shops, to the school garden) and activities (e.g. observing the growth of vegetables, buying food, manipulating and comparing various sizes, shapes, textures, measuring quantities, co-operative work, multi-lingual talk), all of which enable children to develop many scientific, mathematical, social, and linguistic insights.

We would also tend to favour the selection of multi-purpose, flexible and 'transformable' materials and equipment as opposed to single-purpose, 'finished' play resources which can often act as a barrier against the child's imagination and creativity. For instance, Lego in its many varieties, and clay with its infinite possibilities are resources which respond to children's developing imagination and abilities as well as to their changing moods and interests. It is also preferable not to 'crowd' play-areas with a surfeit of commercially-produced toys: real objects and natural materials might also occupy an important place in the learning environment, and parents as well as local markets, shops and community groups are significant resources in terms of such things as fabrics, musical instruments, cooking ingredients and utensils, and a wide variety of domestic objects.

Finally, the community is also, potentially, a rich source of skills that could greatly enhance the quality of learning offered by the class-based curriculum. Visitors like story-tellers, artists, craftspersons, musicians and singers can add fresh, novel, and exciting dimensions to children's experiences.

A holistic approach also implies relating the learning environment of the school to the learning environment of the home, not merely at the outset of the child's schooling, but on a regular, on-going basis. For instance, in the realm of literacy - an area where parents are particularly active with their children - the child is first introduced to the narrative conventions of his/her language in the context of a shared cultural world of meanings and experiences with his/her parents.

This is a *continuous* process and does not cease on the child's entry into mainstream education. Without an on-going knowledge of these experiences, it might be difficult for the teacher to motivate or sustain the child's interest in the literary forms provided by the school. Once again, this and other aspects of the curriculum (as we shall explore more fully in the next Chapter) might be seen as part of a wider process of interaction between children, teachers, and parents.

This approach also means a high level of initiative, imagination, and creativity on the part of teachers since, presently, resources covering the range of learning needs of the developing child are unlikely to be available. Much original material might need to be produced through collaboration with children, parents, and community.

A frequently neglected learning resource is the environment *outside* the school. Indeed, is the distinction between inside and outside really meaningful? As Pamela Mays advises us "We should remember that, to the child, there is only one environment - his, or her, own. The real mystery lies in why the world outside school was ever excluded from the classroom" (Mays, 1985, p.8).

For children, the activities of observing, describing, comparing, and assessing aspects of the immediate surroundings of the school (e.g. streets, shops, buildings, landmarks) constitute highly motivating learning, not only because of their 'real-life' dimension but also on account of the *familiarity of the context*: This is where most children live, accompany their families to the mosque or the market, play with sisters, brothers, and friends, go on outings to parks, fairs, and cinemas, and use a variety of modes of travel.

It is certainly possible to see this environment as a whole 'curriculum' in itself. Children form concepts from images created out of the material the senses provide, and the classroom cannot match the richness, exuberance and variety of life outside school. At the same time, the skills learnt in the classroom can help children to order and refine what they experience outside it.

The importance of the natural environment for the development of scientific skills is well recognised. Direct contact with a variety of natural materials, plants, and animals enhances growth of observation, pattern seeking, and classification skills. In this respect, field-trips should always be preceded by discussion with children about where they are going, why they are going there, what they are going to do; and on return exploration of materials brought back, further discussion and observation, e.g. of a plant, studied from its birth to its death. Once again, the teacher's role in this process of guided observation is vital if children are to make the learning 'connections' (Hale, 1988).

These experiences can also heighten children's awareness of life-sustaining processes and the interdependence of human life and natural life. In this way, they contribute to the development of a sense of wonder and to the growth of the child's reflective inner life. This early awareness of the subtle aspects of existence, of a realm of meaning beyond the tangibly material, greatly enhances the child's inner strength, enabling the growth of moral and co-operative abilities. Indeed, consciousness of a 'spiritual' dimension may well have lasting cognitive benefits, enabling the child to gain deeper insights into the increasingly complex modes of learning he/she will encounter.

The outside world presents children with a unique abundance of natural materials, colours and movements, all of which are essential to the creative process. An environment of rocks and shells, creatures and bones, leaves and birds, grasses and earth, plants and animals, print and images, colours and people, provide the rich sensory experiences out of which may grow a vivid, creative imagination, filled with artistic possibilities.

# Chapter 7
# LEARNING PROCESSES (I):

## Play, Language, Stories
## and Being Bilingual

*Every increase in knowledge is*
*dangerous without a corresponding*
*increase in wisdom  -  Gandhi*

We have so far outlined an initial curriculum model consistent
with the developmental needs of the child and guided by a
positive social philosophy.  We then identified the various
dimensions of the environment with which the child interacts
through active use of existing skills and knowledge to achieve
growth as a motivated, thinking, and self-confident learner.
We emphasised the role of the teacher whose ability to act as
the interpreter of children's home experiences and guide to
their school learning were crucial to children's educational enhancement and rested on the development of a meaningful and
equal relationship with parents.

We also suggested that, for the young child, play is from the
earliest age, 'meaningful' in the sense that it is directed out-
wards, at making sense of the real world.  It is thus intrinsi-
cally bound up with learning and the next two chapters will
look at the increasingly complex levels of learning which in-
teractional play enables.

Corinne Hutt has suggested that all children's play activities
can be essentially divided into two categories: "epistemic play"
(or, "play-for-learning") and "ludic play" (or, "play-for-fun").
(Chazan et al. op. cit)  Epistemic play is essentially related to
the development of cognitive skills and includes problem-
solving (e.g. jigsaw puzzles, constructional toys), exploratory
(e.g. manipulation for materials such as sand, clay, dough), and
productive activities (i.e. when the child ends up with a concrete product - for instance a painting); she also adds that in
the course of exploring and problem-solving, particularly with
a new material or piece of equipment, the child may need help

from the adult to understand the full potential of the object.

Ludic play, on the other hand, is essentially symbolic and fantasy play involving the use of representational objects (e.g. domestic objects or dressing-up clothes for role-play) and the performing of repetitive actions (e.g. acting out the parts of heroine or space adventurer); Hutt also suggests that this kind of play tends to exclude adults and that it is, moreover, less productive in terms of learning gains.

Such a view reflects rather more the dominant status of cognitive, problem-solving skills within early childhood education than the reality of children's play experiences. It ultimately derives from Piaget who was primarily interested in play in terms of its contribution to children's developing intellectual abilities and who largely ignored the emotional and social gains it confers. This in itself was the expression of a specifically eurocentric ideology, very much in keeping with the traditional emphasis, in western society, on the cultivation of cognitive, intellectual, and individualistic skills to the detriment of co-operative and imaginative skills.

Hutt's undervaluing of ludic play can be criticized on a number of grounds: In the first place, many play sequences contain both "epistemic" and "ludic" aspects. A child might, for instance, make a particular shape, form, or model and then invent and act out an imaginative play sequence for its use; indeed children sometimes think up an imaginative play activity and then set about creating the toys that would enable them to derive maximum enjoyment from the activity.

Nor is imaginative play necessarily exclusive of adult participation: very often children at least *offer* adults a role in their play scheme; and research evidence suggests that teachers who enjoy play are welcomed by the children into their games and are often able to extend it by providing new materials or injecting fresh ideas (Chazan et al, op. cit).

Moreover, imaginative play is not 'simply' play-for-fun. It is vital in term of the child's ability to develop a range of social skills and values. It has, for instance, been observed that children who have learned to see the other child's point of view (or to 'decentre') through role play are more likely to attempt to resolve conflicts through verbal rather than physical means. (Chazan et. al. op. cit). This is one of the most crucial social skills and is also related to the moral ability to empathise with other people.

Through imaginative play children create their own meaningful situations which allows them to initiate, reflect, experiment, practice, and negotiate at their own pace. Once again, adults' sensitivity towards their intentions, ideas, and feelings and their ability to 'draw out' the learning aspects of these situations help children link what they are doing, thinking, and feeling with what others are doing, thinking, and feeling. Other learning gains associated with fantasy play include greater self-control, increased social co-operation, reduced restlessness, better concentration, as well as language development. This kind of play, enables the child to imagine and project beyond his/her experiences, and the need to communicate these 'projections' to both other children and adults motivates a great deal of talk. As a result, imaginative play has also been related to an increase in both verbal fluency and story-telling skills.

'Talk' is indeed a major vehicle for learning. While children's all-round development is in the first place dependent upon their own direct play activities and experiences, dialogue, talk with both adults and other children about these activities is an essential condition for effective learning. What others say helps children to structure, interpret, and deepen their experiences.

This process begins, of course, at home, since the child forms his/her initial view of the world at a very early stage. This happens as a result of the primary process of *naming* through which the child establishes relationships and connections with his/her immediate environment - people, objects, places, events. And it is also through this process that children become aware of themselves as unique individuals and develop feelings and values which unite them with family and community.

*Language is therefore both skill and value, both thought and feeling, both experience and interpretation. It is a means of communication, a tool for thinking, a calligraphical art, a memory store, as well as a core cultural value.*

To the young child language is initially meaningful because it is "embedded" in contexts and experiences that are significant to him/her: "The child's awareness of what he/she talks *about* - the things out there to which the language refers - normally takes precedence over his/her awareness of what he/she talks *with* - the words that he/she uses" (Donaldson, op. cit, p.88).

She goes on to argue that success in *our education system*, (Our italics) however, depends on children's ability to *direct* their own thought processes - i.e. to choose words, to reflect upon them, to weigh possible interpretations, in a word, to develop a capacity for abstract thinking. In order to achieve this, children need to become aware of language as a "separate structure, freeing it from its embeddedness in events" (Ibid, p.89).

There is a fine balance to be maintained here: The ability to reflect, to create new worlds out of words through moving away from their immediate context are clearly essential learning tools. If children are to develop their range of potential human skills, they need to be helped to think about their experiences, and to use their imaginations to go beyond these immediate experiences.

However, abstract thought is meaningful only to the extent that it deepens and intensifies the understanding and knowledge of human experience, not as an end-in-itself. There is a fear that an uncritical view of "our education system" (i.e. of 'the way things are') might also imply an acceptance of the dominant, abstract and decontextualized modes of learning and success that it promotes. The value of abstract thought lies in the ability to refer one's thinking constantly back to the concrete situation. The teacher, then, must help children "build bridges which will take them both away from the context and back to it, so that abstract thinking and concrete experiences are permanently linked" (Blenkin and Kelly, op. cit, p.19).

Building bridges, however, demands knowledge of both banks. Adults need first of all to understand the "concrete experiences" which initially shape the child's language and which it also reflects before taking him/her beyond the given, present context. Since language and thought development are so closely inter-related, the way language issues are addressed in the context of a multi-lingual society is a particularly significant feature of education in the early years.

According to the Linguistic Minorities Project survey, carried out between 1979 and 1983, the main languages of Britain other than English, Welsh, Irish/Gaelic and Scottish/Gaelic are now:

| | | |
|---|---|---|
| Arabic | Gujarati | Portuguese |
| Bengali | Hindi | Spanish |
| Cantonese | Italian | Turkish |
| Caribbean Creoles | Panjabi | Ukranian |
| Greek | Polish | Urdu |

(Linguistic Minorities Project, 1985)

The 1987 ILEA Language census recorded 172 languages spoken by school children in the ten inner London divisions, with 23% of the school population using a language other than or in addition to English in the home, an increase of 9% in six years. Fourteen languages had more than 1000 speakers each (Figure 2). The census also shows that bi-lingual children represent approximately 24% of five year olds in all ILEA schools.

Many children therefore start nursery with skills in a mother-tongue other than English, some with differing levels of ability in two or more languages, others possessing equal early fluency in two languages.

However, even advanced thinking in this area (very little of which has permeated into practice) seems to rest on the doubtful assumption that all bilingual children have similar linguistic experiences and will achieve fluency in both languages with relative ease. This denies the reality of 'monolingual' pressures which bear upon the child's home environment, and to which different parents react differently. As a result, little effort is generally made to assess where the child is at in his/her mother-tongue or to distinguish between early 'balanced' (i.e. children with approximately equal skills in two languages) and 'unbalanced' (i.e. children with uneven skills in both languages) biiguals. The potentially serious concequences

FIGURE 2

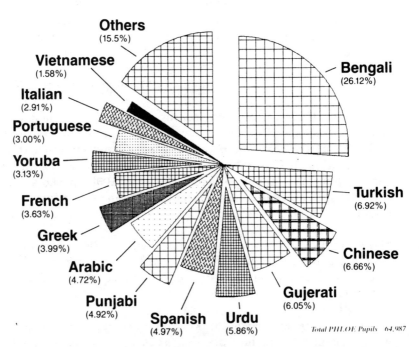

**Others** (15.5%)
**Vietnamese** (1.58%)
**Italian** (2.91%)
**Portuguese** (3.00%)
**Yoruba** (3.13%)
**French** (3.63%)
**Greek** (3.99%)
**Arabic** (4.72%)
**Punjabi** (4.92%)
**Spanish** (4.97%)
**Urdu** (5.86%)
**Gujerati** (6.05%)
**Chinese** (6.66%)
**Turkish** (6.92%)
**Bengali** (26.12%)

*Total PHLOE Pupils 64,987*

**SOURCE: ILEA RESEARCH & STATISTICS 1987**

of this situation have been pointed out by Cummins who on the basis of his research has argued that:

> 'there may be a threshold level of linguistic competence which a bilingual child must attain both in order to avoid cognitive deficits and allow the potentially beneficial aspects of becoming bilingual to influence his/her cognitive growth.'

(Baker, 1988, p.25)

Such an approach to non-English mother-tongues is not, however, altogether surprising in view of the fact that with the exception of some parts of Wales, genuine bilingual learning (i.e. equal development of both the child's languages) continues not to be on the agenda in early years provisions. In current practice, approaches that are termed 'bilingual' are little more than enlightened variations on traditional English-as-a-second-language techniques, with the development of English as the central motivating objective.

Such a model has been described as 'transitional bilingual education' in which the child's first language is only valued to the degree that it serves as a medium for the learning of English, gradually becoming obsolete as the dominant or mainstream language 'takes over'. This assimilationist model is common to both England and USA.

In contrast, 'enrichment bilingual education' as in Wales and Canada seeks to ensure that the child develops equal ease in both his/her languages through provision of human resources (i.e. mother-tongue teachers), materials (e.g. storybooks, songs, rhymes, listening tapes), collaborative teaching, and close home/school partnership. This pluralist enrichment model has, however, yet to see the light of day in England.

Cummins' 'threshold-level hypothesis' - i.e. the view that children with a 'high' threshold level of ability in their first language are more likely to attain a similar level in their second language, with considerable resulting cognitive and social gains - suggests that in many cases initial emphasis in early years would need to be on the development of the child's mother-tongue rather than, as at present, on the learning of English.

It needs to be emphasized that research on children with two or more languages has hardly got off the ground in Britain (a 'structural' effect of racism). Still, the meagre findings that have emerged so far do add weight to Cummins' argument.

The Mother Tongue and English Teaching Project (MOTET) carried out in Bradford between 1978 and 1981 set out to examine the linguistic and more general educational effects of teaching two different groups of Panjabi-speaking South Asian children from working-class backgrounds, an identical reception-class curriculum, one entirely through the medium of English, the other, half through Panjabi and half through English.

Consciousness of the attitudinal context meant that both languages were treated equally in the bilingual programme, i.e. neither language was presented as *the* medium of teaching. Parents were also supportive of the programme, on cultural rather than educational grounds being "uncertain about the linguistic/educational arguments for or against a bilingual programme" (Fitzpatrick, 1987, p.35). The project was, finally, well resourced. Each group was allocated four adults (i.e. 2 teachers and 2 nursery nurses each).

The findings showed that the children who experienced the bilingual programme performed significantly better than the other group in Panjabi and slightly better in English. There was also evidence that *a higher level of performance in Panjabi could transfer to more complex English tasks* (Our italics - Ibid, p.82). It seems that the bi-lingual group greatly benefited from being able to deal with school learning in their first language, simultaneously extending both their linguistic and cognitive skills.

Moreover, evaluations of a wide range of trans-national and cross-cultural early years school programmes have established the beneficial effects of teaching the "language of early cognition" in close conjunction with the "language of education" (Alladina, 1985). In Britain, however, experiments like MOTET have not been repeated, and the DES, LEAs and

Teacher Training institutions have continued to ignore the wealth of cross-cultural research indicating the numerous all-round advantages of balanced bilingualism*, some of which are:

- an earlier and greater awareness of the fact that names are arbitrarily assigned to objects and are subject to change

- earlier separation of meaning from sound

- greater adeptness at creative and divergent thinking (i.e. thoughts and responses that are varied, elaborate, and original rather than simply 'correct')

- greater sensitivity to emotional expressions (e.g. the ability to interpret facial expressions, gestures, intonation, varying situations)

- greater social sensitivity (i.e. the ability to interpret the fine details of each social situation and to react appropriately)

- greater facility in concept formation

(Baker, op. cit.)

One of the effects of this situation may well be that many children are denied the ability to transfer their understanding from 'embedded' to 'disembedded' contexts.

*with obvious consequences on school practice. Some community groups have set up their own bilingual nurseries, e.g. the Latin American Mafalda Nursery in South London. As always, however, resources are a problem.

This process, as we have already suggested, is crucial. The child's movement from the concrete to the abstract and back to a richer concrete identifies the essence of his/her development as a learner. Play interactions with an environment of children, adults, and materials enables the exploring child to move from the 'here and now' uses of language to the reflective worlds of possibilities and interpretations which underlie the acquisition of literacy skills.

Once again, sensitive inputs by teachers and carers, choosing the most appropriate modes of stimulation, are necessary to guide and facilitate this process. One such mode might well be *stories*, which are an essential feature of the child's early learning in the home and the educational potential of which has traditionally been undervalued in early years.

In most provisions the telling or reading of stories is time-tabled at the end of the session, being looked upon as a relaxation from the serious business of 'discovery' learning. There are, however, strong arguments for a more dynamic approach to story-telling in view of the fact that all children potentially make a range of educational gains from stories:

- personal and emotional gains i.e., enjoyment, making sense of their own experiences, identifying with their own language and culture, developing feelings and insights about themselves

- social gains, ie., gaining insight into other people's experiences and cultures, thoughts and emotions. Also, through awareness of story 'audience', acquiring the ability to function as part of a group

- language gains, i.e. gaining awareness of the importance of speech in conveying meaning, as well as new vocabulary and an extension of the range of meanings of familiar words. Also, the gaining of indispensable reading 'cues', i.e. learning to match sounds with pictures, to re-tell story, and an awareness that print contains interesting information

- cognitive gains, i.e. reflecting on their own lives, fantasising about different worlds, understanding of new concepts through the concretely visual nature of their presence in stories, thus extending children's knowledge of the world, and giving them access to new ideas and experiences; also, development of powers of concentration, observation, and memory

(Hester, 1983)

A multi-lingual classroom would need to choose stories that can be told or read in the children's different languages, and the weekly organisation of activities would need to plan for several story-telling sessions, including possible repeats. It is also worth considering whether *all* the children need to listen to *all* the stories: story-time might be staggered with teachers or carers selecting particular sessions as the main, or 'sharing' ones, and allowing children to choose whether or not they wished to participate in the other sessions.

As a concrete example, let us look at a story-telling activity which we have successfully used in the past. The particular story is the hugely popular _Where's Spot,_ by Eric Hill (the hardback version, which is stronger and sturdier), although all the 'Spot' stories are excellent in this context, especially for younger children. It is used in a nursery class of 3 and 4 years olds containing a number of Indian children who are at varying levels of ability in either Urdu or Hindi, and only one child (a girl called Hasina) is a balanced bilingual - her English is almost as developed as her Urdu. The story has been chosen on account of its:

- relatedness to children's home experiences of narrative

- large, clear, colourful, illustrations which make narration easy to follow

- simple language, which allows repetition of key words

- active participatory nature: the open-and-close illustrations which invite the children to 'look for' Spot, are an excellent curiosity-awakening device

The story is told in two sessions: in the morning in Urdu/Hindi (which are almost identical at the level of speech) and in English in the afternoon. All the children participate (in two concurrent groups) in the afternoon session, with all the Indian children and a number of others who have chosen to, taking part in the morning.

After the morning session, props in the form of cut-out figures (with magnetic tape) of the animals and objects in the story, together with a magnetic board, are left available for the children to use. Hasina excitedly leads a younger Indian child towards the props and together they run through and 're-tell' the story (not quite in the original narrative order!), thinking through the sequences and arranging and re-arranging the props on the board as they do so. This collaborative activity also entails the use of additional Urdu/Hindi words to the ones used to tell the story and the imagining of new situations, and it is significant that throughout, the older and more fluent Hasina leads and initiates.

Following the afternoon story, a game which extends the theme of finding something which is hidden is played with all the children. A small model of 'Spot', the dog, has been made with yellow modelling material and a range of objects from the home corner and small construction area (box, covered pan, teapot, open-and-shut lego van, posting-box etc) are used to hide him in. The children are gathered around a table and are given a turn each at 'guessing' in which 'object' Spot is hiding. The game gives rise to a great deal of talk, suspense and excitement.

The morning story-telling session leads to an opportunity for some of the children to practice and develop through collaborative talk their own particular language skills; while other children gain awareness that this is an important and meaningful event in the normal day-to-day life of the nursery 'community'. This process also gives rise to a 'play partnership' between Hasina and her younger friend who is thus at the same time introduced to the value of imaginative play.

The afternoon session allows the latter group to practice their own developing language skills through listening and talking, but also exposes the other children to English. When these children 'meet' the English version they already have the shape, characters and events of the story 'in their heads', which

greatly facilitates access to the new language. It is also important that the process should end with a shared activity, the
turn-taking nature of which promotes a sense of common
belonging to the classroom community.

The morning session will also have confirmed the Indian
children's positive feelings about their language and culture,
thus serving to reinforce links with family and community.
And what results in emotional gains for these children also
results in social gains for the other children through their
awareness of valued cultural differences and their exposure to
a new linguistic experience.

At the same time the children are also enhancing their observation, thinking and memory skills (which could be informally
'assessed' at a subsquent session), as well as their spatial
awareness through the repetition of words like 'behind',
'inside', 'in', 'under' and both the visual (representational) and
real-life illustrations of their meaning. It is also possible,
finally, that at least some of the children will also be developing divergent thinking abilities through observing that similar
meanings can be conveyed by different sound patterns (e.g.
door = *darvaza,* bed = *palang,* etc).

# Chapter 8
# LEARNING PROCESSES (II):
## Stories, Literacy, Mathematics, History and Geography . . .

We have seen how stories can create a wealth of talk amongst children. The spontaneous, authentic 'scripts' which arise during these story-related situations do much to enhance children's literate dispositions. Indeed, for the young child, oral story is the main bridge through which he/she gains access to the 'possible worlds' of abstract thought and language disengaged from its immediate context - the language of print and fiction (Whitehead, 1988)

In this context, the *choice* of stories and the way they are presented are particularly important. Imaginative stories, creating a sense of wonder and excitement are most likely to promote an active engagement with print. A variety of plots, situations, characters, and settings, positively reflecting the multi-cultural dimensions of children's experiences should also be presented since each story offers something a little different to the child.

The value of large, clear illustrations has repeatedly been emphasised since pictures "form the bridge between the contextualized conversation with which the child is so familiar and the decontextualized story where meaning has to be built up from the words alone" (Money, 1988, p.151). Reading development is further enhanced when there is the right balance between familiar and unfamiliar words in the story and when initially, narratives bear some relationship to the familiar flow of the child's speech (Donaldson, op. cit).

Finally, there are different ways of presenting stories: reading through books, telling through props, relating through tape. The latter provides opportunities for children to listen to stories without the aid of pictures: regular experience of 'making sense' from words alone, coming through the spoke voice with all the added cues to meaning which changes of tone and musicality can bring is immensely valuable to the young reader.

Some writers distinguish between "emergent reading" i.e. the time when the child is simply aware that print carries a message and can recognize some of the visual characteristics of the print specific to his/her language, (through handling books at home, seeing their own and other family members' names written down) and "early reading", when the child begins to perceive the precise correspondence between spoken and written language (Money, op. cit). There is, however, general agreement that the thrill of story, and the practical activities that flow from it - collaborative talk, listening, re-telling, imaginative play - are the primary motivating drives for learning to read.

*Success* in reading, however, depends on adults enabling children to use their own linguistic resources and experiences in making sense of print. If the language they are reading is unfamiliar and if the events, situations, and concepts described are outside their experience, 'making sense' may prove to be an exhausting and discouraging experience for children. On the other hand, if the world described in the story is known to the child this may in itself provide the motivation to tackle new features of the language.

Initially, reading may be seen as the "shared exploration" of a text (Blenkin and Kelly, op. cit. p.40) with either the adult or an older, more experienced child reading alongside the beginner. Setting aside time to hear the child read and supporting his/her search for meaning are particularly important. In this context, the key role may well be that of parents whose advantage over teachers here comes in the fact that they are potentially able to engage in textual 'negotiations of meaning' with the child at a significantly deeper level than the teacher.

However recent research also suggests, disturbingly, that multiple indices of social deprivation affect parents' ability to support their children's learning (ILEA, 1988). A Sheffield study found that the presence of three or more adverse social factors (unemployment, poor health, bad housing) negatively influences a child's home reading frequency (Weinberger, 1986).

The *process* of becoming an able and self-confident reader once again involves a partnership in which teacher and parent work together to enhance the child's assurance in handling print. One example of this is the PACT (Parent and Children and Teachers) scheme which was launched throughout Hackney in 1981, aimed at involving parents in helping their children to read. The ILEA has recently evaluated this scheme: Researchers found that the most successful children were those who read regularly to their parents and whose parents had regular contact with teachers; they also observed that PACT was most successful in schools where it was an integral part of the educational philosophy of the school and where heads were enthusiastic and staff had collaboratively discussed the implications at some length i.e. where it was just one part of a whole school literacy policy (ILEA, 1988).

*Writing* is an expression of literacy, but it is more than just a linguistic skill, as it is both language and representation. Vygotsky has argued that the origins of writing lie in the child's symbolic and imaginative play (Vygotsky, 1978) which, by allowing him/her to replace a real object with an image or a symbol which stands for the object helps create the early dispositions towards writing. This yet again illustrates the importance, referred to earlier, of imaginative play. It emphasises the value of facilitating experiences of a wide range of representations which enable children to move from their first personal concepts to 'public modes'.

Through story-related activities, children engage in 'language-linked' role-play, reflect on words, converse, perceive and feel print, while dance, drama, 'small world', and outdoor play enable them to develop their understandings of movement, gesture, shape and configuration. A great deal of significance is also placed on the child's early drawing and mark-making which is seen as the achievement of a complex representational skill: making traces through body action (Mathews, 1988).

In learning to write, therefore, children make full use of the range of their developing skills. The *desire* to write, however, only occurs when the child has 'something to say' (i.e. the will to create, or to "compose") as well as some degree of knowledge of the writing conventions of his/her language (the skill to represent, or to "transcribe"). It has also been suggested that it is only when children feel that they have something to say that they will fully engage in learning transcription skills (Money, op. cit).

Reading to children also takes on an added significance here, allowing them to be introduced to the rules of print, directionality, spacing and storybook conventions. Children often first become aware of the significance of print by recognizing and using those letters which make up their own name. However, they may not do so at school unless they feel comfortable and secure, and unless the learning invironment is well resourced, especially when they come with languages and scripts other than English. Once again the role of teachers in this interaction is vitally significant. How can they create the conditions which will allow the shaping of children's literary creativity?

In this respect a collection of articles by teachers from the ILEA Writing Project, describing their work in multi-cultural classrooms between 1986 and 1987 makes fascinating reading. They identified the following conditions as essential in promoting the 'write(!) environment':

- *a stimulating and varied environment* in which children are surrounded by as many different forms of print as possible, and by a wide variety of writing equipment. This arouses *curiosity* and enables children to ask questions, explore, discover, and become aware of writing as an important and useful activity.

- *a relaxed, informal atmosphere* which makes learning to write enjoyable and voluntary, and which gives children the time, freedom and confidence to discover writing for themselves.

- *co-operative work*, i.e. children, teachers, and parents working together in the classroom. This allows children and adults who share a first language other than English to work together and to use both languages, whether the writing is in the child's first language or in English. Moreover, encouraging children to read and write together enables them to learn from each other; while teachers can learn more by working alongside a child or by acting as 'scribe' for the ideas of a group of children, rather than by simply receiving completed pieces of writing by children.

- *imaginative play situations* (cooking, shop, restaurant, drama, celebrations) which encourage children to use their literacy skills in a socially meaningful context.

(The National Writing Project in ILEA, 1988)

One Teacher describes an experience with his class of 3 and 4 year olds:

*"In attempting to encourage writing with a biliteral slant, a trip to Chinatown was arranged for a small group of nursery children. The idea was to have a day out, visit a Chinese restaurant, and bring back props and food so as to set up our own restaurant in the nursery. We also took many photographs during our visit. These photographs were later turned into a tape slide, on which the commentary was set out by the children themselves. This was then shown to all the children in the nursery and used as another classroom resource.*

*We hoped that from this trip, the bilingual children (especially the Cantonese speaking children) would become more involved in the developing role play. As props, we provided menus, all types of writing implements, books to write in, including diaries. Some junior children also decorated the windows of our restaurant, using Chinese writing. We hoped that the monolingual children's interest in other languages would be increased by coming into contact with written Chinese. We hoped too that the Chinese children would use their home language, both spoken and written while taking part in role play in the restaurant.*

*To a certain extent this did happen. The Cantonese speaking children did spend proportionately more time in the restaurant than they had done in other areas of role play, they also used their home language more openly. We followed this up by cooking Chinese food, using authentic Chinese recipes. And on one occasion a parent of one of the Chinese children gave a struggling teacher a helping hand.*

*Then an exciting development took place. The children's work began to show elements of other scripts. A couple of the Chinese children were including elements of Chinese script in their writing. Both Chinese and English seemed to be developing side by side. There were also examples of work in Tamil appearing from a child in my class. And monolingual English children were beginning to include Chinese writing in their work."*

(Ibid)

This philosophy marks a radical departure from the 'traditional' (monolingual) approach to literacy characterised by the use of reading schemes, phonics in reading and spelling, and an emphasis on correctness in writing (transcription) over content (composition). In this approach children generally work individually using exercise books and in competition with one another, parents are safely kept out of the classroom, and it is the teacher who decides what children read or write about.

In contrast, the 'developmental' approach outlined above attempts to make reading and writing enjoyable, motivating children by focussing on their particular linguistic skills, their experiences and interests. Children and teachers together decide what to read and write about, and the emphasis is on creativity rather than correctness. Children may work in various ways - individually, in pairs, in groups, as a class, co-operating with one another - as well as with teachers and parents. This perspective understands writing not simply as a means of communication but also as *part of* thinking, feeling, and cultural identity*.

*This approach however, does not necessarily in itself promote an 'enrichment' model of bilingual education. It may be perfectly compatible with an assimilationist 'transitional' model.

The developmental approach, has so far been most extensively used in the London Borough of Hackney, spearheaded by the Literacy Development Team set up in 1984. Evaluation carried out by an ILEA team of researchers found that teachers using this method as opposed to the traditional one were more successful in raising the performance of low-achieving children, while those children who approached literacy 'developmentally' overall made the most progress (ILEA, 1988).

As is the case with language, the child's early learning is also 'naturally mathematical'. We have seen that for the young child, play is perpetual exploration, through his or her senses, of the *spaces* around him/her, and of how things exist both in relation to each other and in relation to the child. In the home the child also develops a wealth of experience contrasting, comparing and matching many different objects, shapes, textures, and colours. And he/she will also have seen, heard, and talked about numbers (associated, for instance, with time) in natural, everyday situations.

Early awareness of space, shape, measure and number is enhanced through the child's active investigation of concrete materials in the school environment. Well-resourced home-corner and construction play, for instance, can develop concepts of shape and size, while cooking lends itself to a great many mathematical discoveries - e.g. understanding of quantity, weight, measure, texture, as well as shape and size. Moreover, in manipulating objects, exploring and matching sets of things, counting and recounting the objects within the sets, and talking about these experiences, the child begins to learn that 'counting words' can also be used to describe a set, i.e. that "the number of objects in a set becomes a way of describing that set mathematically" (Metz, 1988, p.194). This once again, enables the child to move from knowledge based on concrete experience to the symbolic descriptive language specific to mathematics.

The teacher's guidance and support is, in this respect, all-important. Involvement with the child in play situations 'with mathematical possibilities' and conversation and discussion emphasising mathematical properties and relationships (e.g. "How many more ... do we need?") are essential. Once again, stories and rhymes involving numbers can be a significant learning aid: by locating abstract sums in concrete, social contexts, they help children make sense of them. As with other aspects of the curriculum, the child's development of mathematical concepts can most easily be fostered in situations which have meaning and interest for him/her.

Teachers need to be aware, however, that children potentially bring several languages of early mathematical perception into the classroom. These should be understood and valued as the foundation of each child's learning. And it might prove an interesting challenge for teachers to learn the 1 to 10 count in their children's different languages.

We have suggested that play and the daily routines of the home convey a strong sense of both space and time to the young child. Moreover, through talk, conversation with adults, children very early on learn to order their own mental processes in terms of time, or to 'speak in narrative'; while even before the child can walk, he/she must prepare a 'map' of his/her environment using mental abilities as well as senses of sight and touch. These understandings are initially, of course, 'context-bound' and, once again, adults need to provide the educational filters that would enable children to move from sense-linked knowledge to a comprehension of the social concepts of time and place, of 'history' and 'geography'.

The mention of 'narrative' brings us back, once again, to the potential of stories as 'bridge' between the child's own concrete experiences of time and place and the more complex, associative thinking required to gain historical and geographical insights.

Stories are always told or written in time, they have a beginning, a middle and an end; they are "pieces of miniature history" (Mays, op. cit. p.117). Stories are also always set in a particular spatial context, real or imaginary. They are, it can be said, in accord with some of the basic inner processes of the child. But there are also stories *about* Time and *about* Place. Such stories are always, moreover, concerned with *diversity*. Time stories introduce children to different people in different places at different times in the past. Place stories introduce them to different people in different places today. Thus children are helped to become aware of how different and how similar they are from other people and ages which helps them broaden their experience of the world (Blyth, 1984)

Once again, this process begins in the home where parents, grandfather or grandmother thrill the child with oral accounts of their own childhood and past experiences, their knowledge of, or participation in, culturally significant local or historical events, in a variety of places. The stories, aneodotes, memories and reminiscences of the home together with visits to and from relatives living far away, convey to the child his/her initial sense of a culturally meaningful history and geography. The child thus becomes aware, that time and place are not just part of his/her life, but part of others' lives as well. Children begin to understand that time and place also exist *outside* of their experience of it, and begin to see themselves as part of a collective and continuing pattern of living. We have seen how this ability to decentre is crucial to the child's acquisition of social, moral, language, literacy and mathematical skills. It is equally fundamental in promoting the understanding of historical and geographical concepts.

Discussion between children and with teachers about stories, teachers constantly referring back to events and places to ensure learning gains, and relating these events and places to children's real experiences, all advance the process of understanding. Moreover, story-related imaginative play which allows children to 'travel' both 'in time' and to different 'places', to make their own models and constructions and to describe and share these experiences through talk, progressively enable them to acquire the language of historical and geographical thinking. Children can also further explore their own interests through history and geography reference books reflecting a wide variety of eras, lands, and cultures. And these topics can also motivate a thirst for reading as well as a great deal of creative writing.

An interesting practical activity to motivate children's explorations is the 'Family Tree' which involves collaboration between children, teachers, and parents and which also presents an integrated approach to Time and Place. Old objects, artefacts, photographs, newspaper cuttings belonging to the family or brought back from recent travel are also excellent resources and may have added relevance for other areas of the curriculum.

There are also environmental dimensions to children's learning about Time and Place which acquire an ever increasing significance in early years as they provide first-hand evidence of patterns and relationships, contrasts and comparisons, differences and similarities. Fieldwork could range from a simple stepping-out into the school playground to study weather, a walk in the country involving the study of soil, a visit to a particular street or locality, to a museum, art-gallery or a building of historical interest.

Time and Place is one area of the curriculum which requires well-planned resourcing and a particularly thoughtful approach on the part of the teacher. Resources need to be *meaningful* to children, i.e. to positively reflect the environments, histories and civilizations of their communities; they should also convey the highly significant cross-cultural contribution of women to their histories and societies.

This may be problematic since the (hopefully) positive teacher attitudes and resources of the classroom are potentially contradicted by the negative images of peoples and lands of the sourthern world, as well as of inner-city communities and of women, on much of the media, especially television. And television, as we all know to our costs, exercises a considerable influence on children's perceptions. It is important for the teacher to *create situations* that would enable children to re-interpret some of their perceptions and explore some of their feelings (in relation to violence for instance), in the safe environment of the classroom. And it may be that introducing *some* negative images as part of a well-thought out process of encouraging children to be critical, might sharpen their awareness of the power relations that underlie many public forms of representation, and enable children to make informed moral and aesthetic choices.

These descriptions of children's learning processes do not mean that the child spends all his/her time frenziedly engaged in 'knowing' activities within the classroom. Blenkin and Kelly argue that curriculum planning should allow children to communicate with teachers about feelings aroused by " 'What I can't do' or 'What frightens me'." (Blenkin and Kelly, op. cit. p.39).

Enabling children to come to terms with anxieties and limitations could encourage them to take risks in their learning and progress through experimentation, which implies the right to make 'mistakes'. For instance, teachers can often learn more about children's ideas on writing from what they get wrong, (or 'miscues') rather than from what they get right. The exploring child, therefore, needs to feel good both about his/her strengths and his/her limitations.

We have also suggested the limitations of seeing children's activities purely in terms of end-products which may conceal the range of creative processes occurring within the child and which shape his/her learning. Children need blocks of unpressured time and space to reflect upon experiences and feelings, to take things in, to follow their own thoughts and dream their own dreams, and to know themselves. Exploring a range of sensory experiences, thinking, feeling and imagining, are essential human skills but they cannot be measured in terms of 'productivity'.

For this reason, we have sought to focus on the processes of creativity within the child rather than on points, or stages of achievement. We have presented the child's play-based learning as a unitary model of multi-dimensional activities based on the holistic view that the same things can be seen and understood in a variety of ways - aesthetically, scientifically, mathematically, geographically, historically. This leads to an integrated and developmental view of the curriculum whose dimensions inter-relate and cross-fertilise to produce ever deeper learning opportunities, both for the child and the adult. "Achievements" are, from this perspective, multiple rather than single.

# Chapter 9
# EVALUATION

---

The organic view of both child development and the curriculum that we advocate implies a particular philosophy, or indeed "art" of educational evaluation (Eisner, 1985). In essence this can be described as a *qualitative* method of evaluation, resting on observation-based formative and continuous record-keeping.

This method allows teachers to focus on the meaningful *processes* of curriculum experience in relation to each child, and to provide other adults (parents, other teachers, school governors, inspectors etc) with open, regular information about the development of skills and social abilities. In contrast summative records, based on a 'productivist' view of learning, rely on one-off tests (e.g. standardized achievement tests) which examine what children can produce on one occasion in an isolated setting, based on 'objective', centralized norms.

In Chapter 4 we considered the importance of a child profile, complemented by continuous and sensitive child observations and regular exchange of information with parents. Formative records complete this process: they enable cumulative measurement of each child's progress and also allow teachers to assess and plan both play provision and the organisation of the learning environment so as to ensure that they remain consistent with each child's developing skills. In this way, they also point towards self-evaluation.

In our view, parental input (e.g comparative information or assessments) is an essential element of such records, allowing teachers to relate the child's progress in both learning environments of home and school.*  It also allows parents to regularly monitor their children's progress and to be in a better position to support their learning in the home. Records might

*As an example see the ILEA's *Primary Language Record* featured in the Appendix.

comprise dated samples of children's work as well as observations on, particular play situations and activities; they might also indicate the teacher's view of the *significance* of the particular items chosen in relation to the child's progress.

Evaluation, therefore, implies interpretation. The skill of the teacher lies precisely in discerning when a child's behaviour is developmentally meaningful, how best to record it, what words to use etc. For instance, an episode of imaginative play with no 'end-product' might be developmentally more significant than a painting or a model produced by a child. But the teacher might miss it and decide only to record the tangible products. The 'art' of observing and interacting with children in all areas of the learning environment can once again be seen to be crucial.

Whole school policies, collaborative teaching, effective teamwork, and meaningful staff meetings greatly assist evaluation processes by providing a common frame of reference, shared responsibility, and collective support. These elements are also significant in terms of teacher self-evaluation as they enable the discussion of a range of views on attitudes, cultural values and assumptions, fears, teaching styles, curriculum planning and content. INSET courses also enable the development of thinking and the sharing of ideas with other colleagues. Finally, it is also important for teachers to keep abreast of recent thinking and research on Early Years and to review their practice in that light.

Evaluation and assessment procedures are also, of course, affected by the prevailing political climate within education. In this respect the proposed National Curriculum comes in the form of an alarming package. It emphasises the primacy of the 'core' subjects of English, Mathematics, and Science with clear implications in terms of curriculum planning and time-tabling; it sets out centralized 'attainment targets' for each subject, with initial testing of all children at the age of seven; and it will introduce formal procedures of evaluation, which will also partly serve as 'political' instruments for teacher appraisal. It presents an objective view of knowledge based on subjects 'waiting to be learnt'. And children are, once again, set to become instruments of the State's will.

These propositions are entirely inconsistent with the approach we are advocating and are unlikely to provide teachers with a deeper insight into the patterns of learning of the individual children in their care. And unless this aspect of the process of teaching remains in the forefront, the 'results' apparently aimed for by the government are unlikely to occur.

However, although evaluation procedures will, to some extent, be imposed on schools, the qualitative nature of assessments will continue to be decided by teachers even though these might not exactly 'fit' the form that will be required. In this light, it is important, in our view for teachers to maintain and to strengthen their committment to formative processes of evaluation *within which* they might integrate the authorities summative requirements.

# A FINAL WORD

We have attempted to tell our story in the form of a narrative of relationships. At the heart of this narrative lies the child and his/her growth. The idea of 'Wholeness' that we have sought to explore in relation to the child is certainly not original to ourselves. A very long time ago now, the poet Rabindranath Tagore expressed it with an eloquence that we could not hope to match, when he said:

> *"Growth is the movement of a whole towards a yet fuller wholeness. A child starts with this wholeness from the beginning and is not an unfinished being. Life is a continual process of synthesis, and not of additions."*

(Sahi, 1980, p.25)

In this movement, teachers and carers play a vital role as they create part of the child's formative context. If children are to arrive at this "fuller wholeness", their journey needs to be guided by adults who are deep thinkers themselves, able to visualize the integration of the child's experience across the range of contexts in which he/she explores the world, and to use this vision to motivate the child's further discoveries.

This brings us to the heart of the problem. For if the vision of teachers and carers fails them and if they wilfully ignore or demean any aspect of the child's meaningful context, the child may be set on the road to failure.

Both of these dispositions, lack of imagination and negative attitudes, owe their origins to the set of historical processes that we outlined earlier, which gave rise to the oppressions of racism, class, and gender. The values, ideologies and compartmentalized modes of thinking accompanying the emergence of these social inequalities were continually nurtured by education and other forms of socialization, so that they have become part of the institutional fabric of British society. In present-day Britain they continue to manifest themselves, with renewed vigour.

At the same time, the continuing social inequalities are, after all, human constructs and, as such, can be changed by human will and action. But now a fresh challenge faces those of us who wish to create a better society *with* our children: It is a further challenge of vision - the necessity of seeing the diverse strands of social inequality as inter-related, of refusing to accept its partitioning into single issues and separate causes, of making 'relationships' the basis for all our social and political understandings.

Once again, we can learn from the child who enjoys this advantage over us, that for him/her, knowledge is not - as yet - linear, fragmented, and partitioned, but a holistic aspect of the mind itself. It enables the child to be endlessly inventive and imaginative, to be, in a word, the artist that Jyoti Sahi describes:

> *I give a child a lump of clay. What does the child do? She plays with the clay, feels it, discovers intuitively what clay can do. She then finds to her surprise that she can roll the clay into a long sausage. ...The child is delighted with her discovery. You ask the child what she has made - and she answers immediately 'a snake'. Here we see symbolic thinking working spontaneously. What primordial structure of her mind responded to the structure she had created out of clay, to make of it this metaphor, this symbol? Let us watch the child go further. She finds that by twisting her long snaky line of clay round and round in a spiralling form, she can make a plane. But she can do more. She can spiral her long sausage upwards, making a vessel. This is an invention of great importance - one of the turning points in the history of human civilization: it enabled neolithics to make their first vessel in which they could store things.*

# APPENDIX

## THE ILEA PRIMARY LANGUAGE RECORD

# Primary Language Record

| School | | School Year |
|---|---|---|

| Name | DoB | Summer born child |
|---|---|---|
| | ☐ Boy ☐ Girl | |

| Languages understood | Languages read |
|---|---|
| Languages spoken | Languages written |

| Details of any aspects of hearing, vision or coordination affecting the child's language/literacy. Give the source and date of this information. | Names of staff involved with child's language and literacy development. |
|---|---|

# Part A To be completed during the Autumn Term

**A1 Record of discussion between child's parent(s) and class teacher** *(Handbook pages 12-13)*

*Signed* Parent(s) _____ Teacher _____

Date _____

**A2 Record of language/literacy conference with child** *(Handbook pages 14-15)*

Date _____

# Part B

## Child as a language user (one or more languages)

*(Handbook pages 17-18)*

Teachers should bear in mind the Authority's Equal Opportunities Policies (race, gender and class) in completing each section of the record and should refer to *Educational Opportunities for All?*, the ILEA report on special educational needs.

---

### B1 Talking and listening

*(Handbook pages 19-22)*

Please comment on the child's development and use of spoken language in different social and curriculum contexts, in English and/or other community languages: evidence of talk for learning and thinking; range and variety of talk for particular purposes; experience and confidence in talking and listening with different people in different settings.

What experiences and teaching have helped/would help development in this area? Record outcomes of any discussion with head teacher, other staff, or parent(s).

---

### B2 Reading

*(Handbook pages 23-28)*

Please comment on the child's progress and development as a reader in English and/or other community languages: the stage at which the child is operating (refer to the reading scales on pages 26-27); the range, quantity and variety of reading in all areas of the curriculum; the child's pleasure and involvement in story and reading, alone or with others; the range of strategies used when reading and the child's ability to reflect critically on what is read.

*continued*

77

What experiences and teaching have helped/would help development in this area? Record outcomes of any discussion with head teacher, other staff, or parent(s).

---

**B3 Writing**  *(Handbook pages 29-34)*

Please comment on the child's progress and development as a writer in English and/or other community languages: the degree of confidence and independence as a writer; the range, quantity and variety of writing in all areas of the curriculum; the child's pleasure and involvement in writing both narrative and non-narrative, alone and in collaboration with others; the influence of reading on the child's writing; growing understanding of written language, its conventions and spelling.

What experiences and teaching have helped/would help development in this area? Record outcomes of any discussion with head teacher, other staff, or parent(s).

---

Signature of head teacher and all teachers contributing to this
section of the record:

---

78

# Part C To be completed during the Summer Term*

(Handbook page 35)

**C1 Comments on the record by child's parent(s)**

**C2 Record of language/literacy conference with child**

**C3 Information for receiving teacher**
This section is to ensure that information for the receiving teacher is as up to date as possible. Please comment on changes and development in any aspect of the child's language since Part B was completed.

What experiences and teaching have helped/would help development? Record outcomes of any discussion with head teacher, other staff, or parent(s).

Signed: Parent(s) _____    Class Teacher _____

Date _____    Head Teacher _____

*To be completed by the Summer half-term for 4th year juniors.

79

# Observations and Samples (Primary Language Record)

*attach extra pages where needed*

**Name:**                          Year Group:

## 1 Talking & listening: diary of observations

The diary below is for recording examples of the child's developing use of talk for learning and for interacting with others in English and/or other community languages.

Include different kinds of talk (e.g. planning an event, solving a problem, expressing a point of view or feelings, reporting on the results of an investigation, telling a story ...)

Note the child's experience and confidence in handling social dimensions of talk (e.g. initiating a discussion, listening to another contribution, qualifying former ideas, encouraging others ...)

The matrix sets out some possible contexts for observing talk and listening. Observations made in the diary can be plotted on the matrix to record the range of social and curriculum contexts sampled.

*(Handbook pages 37-39)*

| LEARNING CONTEXTS | pair | small group | child with adult | small/large group with adult | |
|---|---|---|---|---|---|
| collaborative reading and writing activities | | | | | |
| play, dramatic play, drama & storying | | | | | |
| environmental studies & historical research | | | | | |
| maths & science investigations | | | | | |
| design, construction, craft & art projects | | | | | |
| | | | | | |
| | | | | | |
| | | | | | |

SOCIAL CONTEXTS

| Dates | Observations and their contexts |
|---|---|
| | |

©ILEA 1988

## 2 Reading and Writing: diary of observations
(reading and writing in English and/or other community languages)

(Handbook pages 40-44)

| Date | Reading |
|------|---------|
|      | Record observations of the child's development as a reader (including wider experiences of story) across a range of contexts. |

**Writing**

Record observations of the child's development as a writer (including stories dictated by the child) across a range of contexts.

81

## 3 **Reading Samples** (reading in English and/or other community languages)
*to include reading aloud and reading silently* (Handbook pages 45-49)

| Dates | | | |
|---|---|---|---|
| **Title or book/text** (fiction or information) | | | |
| **Known/unknown text** | | | |
| **Sampling procedure used:** informal assessment/running record/miscue analysis | | | |
| **Overall impression of the child's reading:** <br> • confidence and degree of independence <br> • involvement in the book/text <br> • the way in which the child read the text aloud | | | |
| **Strategies the child used when reading aloud:** <br> • drawing on previous experience to make sense of the book/text <br> • playing at reading <br> • using book language <br> • reading the pictures <br> • focusing on print (directionality, 1:1 correspondence, recognition of certain words) <br> • using semantic/syntactic/ grapho-phonic cues <br> • predicting <br> • self-correcting <br> • using several strategies or over-dependent on one | | | |
| **Child's response to the book/text:** <br> • personal response <br> • critical response (understanding, evaluating, appreciating wider meanings) | | | |
| **What this sample shows about the child's development as a reader.** <br><br> **Experiences/support needed to further development.** | | | |

• Early indicators that the child is moving into reading

82

## 4 **Writing Samples** (reading in English and/or other community languages)

*'Writing' to include children's earliest attempts at writing*

(Handbook pages 50-54)

| **Dates** | | | |
|---|---|---|---|
| **Context and background information about the writing:**<br>• how the writing arose<br>• how the child went about the writing<br>• whether the child was writing alone or with others<br>• whether the writing was discussed with anyone while the child was working on it<br>• kind of writing (e.g. list, letter, story, poem, personal writing, information writing)<br>• complete piece of work/extract | | | |
| **Child's own response to the writing.** | | | |
| **Teacher's response:**<br>• to the content of the writing<br>• to the child's ability to handle this particular kind of writing<br>• overall impression | | | |
| **Development of spelling and conventions of writing.** | | | |
| **What this writing shows about the child's development as a writer:**<br>• how it fits into the range of the child's previous writing<br>• experience/support needed to further development | | | |

*Please keep the writing with the sample sheet*

# REFERENCES

ALLADINA, S (1985): *Positive Interaction between the Languages of Early Cognition and the acquisition of the Language of Education. A Report on the Policies and Practice in Multilingual Societies and their Comparison with the Language Teaching Provision in the ILEA.* 1983/4 ILEA Teacher Fellow Report. Centre for Multicultural Education, University of London Institute of Education.

BAKER, C (1988): *Key Issues in Bilingualism and Bilingual Education.* Multilingual Matters Ltd, Avon.

BLENKIN, G.M. and KELLY, A.V. (1988): *Early Childhood Education: A Developmental Curriculum.* Paul Chapman Publishing Ltd, London.

BLYTH, J (1984): *Place and Time with Children Five to Nine.* Croom Helm Ltd, Kent.

BOWER, t (1977): *The Perceptual World of the Child.* Fontana/Open Books, Oxford.

BRUCE, T (1987): *Early Childhood Education.* Hodder and Stoughton Ltd, Kent.

BRUNER, J.S. (1981): *The Pragmatics of Acquisition* in DEUTSCH, W (ed): *The Child's Construction of Language.* Academic Press, London.

CAPRA, F (1982): *The Turning Point. Science, Society, and the Rising Culture.* Wildwood House, London

CENTRAL ADVISORY COUNCIL FOR EDUCATION (England) (1967): *Children and their Primary Schools (The Plowden Report).* HMSO, London

CHAZAN, M, LAING, A, and HARPER, G (1987): *Teaching Five to Eight Year Olds.* Basil Blackwell Ltd, Oxford.

COHEN, B (1988): *Caring for Children: Services and Policies for childcare and Equal Opportunities in the United Kingdom.*

*Report for the European Commission's Childcare Network*. Commission of the European Communities, London.

CURTIS, A.M. (1986): *A Curriculum for the Pre-school Child: Learning to Learn*. Nfer-Nelson, Berkshire.

DELAMONT, S (1980): *Sex Roles and The School*. Methuen and Co. Ltd, London.

DEPARTMENT OF EDUCATION AND SCIENCE/WELSH OFFICE (1975): *A Language For Life (The Bullock Report)*. HMSO, London.

(1981): *West Indian Children in Our Schools (The Rampton Report)*. HMSO, London

(1982): *Mathematics Counts (The Cockroft Report)*. HMSO, London.

(1985): *Education for All (The Swann Report)*. HMSO, London.

(1987): *The National Curriculum 5-16. A Consultation Document*. HMSO, London.

(1988): *The National Curriculum. English for Ages 5-11*. HMSO, London.

DONALDSON, M (1978): *Children's Minds*. Fontana Press, Oxford.

EISNER, E.E. (1986): *The Art of Educational Evaluation: A Personal view*. The Falmer Press, Sussex.

FITZPATRICK, F (1987): *The Open Door: The Bradford Bilingual Project*. Multilingual Matters Ltd, Avon.

HALE, M (1988): *Ecology in The Curriculum: 5-19*. British Ecological Society, York.

HAZAREESINGH, S (1986): *Racism and Cultural Identity: An Indian Perspective* in *Dragon's Teeth*, Number 24, Summer 1986.

HECHTER, M (1975): *Internal colonialism: The Celtic Fringe in*

*British National Development 1536-1966.* Routledge and Kegan Paul, London.

HESTER, H (1983): *Stories in the Multilingual Primary Classroom.* ILEA, Centre for Urban Educational Studies, London.

HURST, V (1988): *Parents and Professionals: Partnership in Early Childhood Education* in BLENKIN and KELLY op. cit.

INNER LONDON EDUCATION AUTHORITY (1987): *Research and Statistics Reports. 1987 Language Census.*

INNER LONDON EDUCATION AUTHORITY (1987): *Research and Statistics Reports. Catalogue of Languages Spoken by ILEA School Pupils.*

INNER LONDON EDUCATION AUTHORITY (1988): *Research and Statistics Reports. The Hackney Literacy Study.*

KAKAR, S (1981): *The Inner World. A psycho-analytic study of Childhood and Society in India.* Oxford University Press, New Delhi.

KEDDIE, N (1971): *Classroom Knowledge* in YOUNG, M.F.D. (ed): *Knowledge and Control.* Collier-Macmillan, London

LINGUISTIC MINORITIES PROJECT (1985): *The Other Languages of England.* Routledge and Kegan Paul, London

MATTHEWS, J (1988): *The Young Child's Early Representation and Drawing* in BLENKIN and KELLY op. cit.

MAYS, P (1985): *Teaching Children through the Environment.* Hodder and Stoughton, London.

METZ. M (1988): *The Development of Mathematical Understanding* in BLENKIN and KELLY op. cit.

MONEY, T (1988): *Early Literacy* in BLENKIN and KELLY op. cit.

MOSS, P (1988): *Childcare and Equality of Opportunity. Consolidated Report to the European Commission.* Commission of the

86

European Communities, London.

NATIONAL WRITING PROJECT IN ILEA (1988): *Working with Bilingual Writers 3-16.*

OSBORN, A.F and MILBANK, J.E (1987): *The Effects of Early Education. A Report from the Child Health and Education Study.* Clarendon Press, Oxford.

REYNOLDS, J and SKILBECK, M (1976): *Culture and the Classroom.* Open Books, London.

SAHI, J (1980): *The Child and the Serpent. Reflections on Popular Indian Symbols.* Routledge and Kegan Paul, London.

SMITH, G. (1985): *Language, Ethnicity, Employment, Education and Research: The Struggle of Sylheti-speaking People in London.* University of London, Institute of Education.

STEDMAN JONES, G (1971): *Outcast London. A study in the Relationship between Classes in Victorian Society.* Peregrine Books, London

TIZARD, B and HUGHES, M (1984): *Young Children Learning.* Fontana, London.

TOWNSEND, P (1987): *Poverty and Labour in London. Interim Report of a Centenary Survey.* Low Pay Unit, London.

TOWNSEND, P (1988): *Inner City Deprivation and Premature Death in Greater Manchester.* Tameside Metropolitan Borough.

VGOTSKY, L(1978): *Mind in Society.* Harvard University Press, Cambridge, Massachussets.

WALKER, A and WALKER C (1987): *The Growing Divide: A Social Audit, 1979-1987.* Child Poverty Action Group, London.

WALLACE, C (1988): *Learning to Read in a Multicultural Society: The Social Context of Second Language Literacy.* Prentice Hall, London.

WEINBERGER, J (1986): *Variation in Take-up of a Project to*

*Involve Parents in The Teaching of Reading* in *Educational Studies* Vol.12, No.2.

WELLS, G (1982): *Influences of the home on language development* in DAVIES, A (ed), *Language and Learning in Home and School.*Heinemann Educational Books, London.

WHITEHEAD, M (1988): *Narrative, Stories and the world of Literature,* in BLENKIN and KELLY, op. cit.

WOLF, D and GARDNER, H (1980): *Beyond Playing or Polishing: A Developmental View of Artistry* in HAUSEMAN, J.J (ed), *Arts and the Schools.* McGraw Hill, New York.

# GENERAL BIBLIOGRAPHY

AIDAROVA L (1982): *Child Development and Education.* Progress Publishers, Moscow.

ANTONOVA, K. BONGARD-LEVIN, G. KOTOVSKI, G (1979): *A History of India.* Progress Publishers, Moscow.

BROWNE, N and FRANCE, P (eds) (1986): *Unitying the Apron Strings: Anti-Sexist provision for the Under-Fives.* Open University Press, Milton Keynes.

BRUNER, J (1966): *Towards a Theory of Instruction.* Harvard University Press, Massachusetts.

BRYAN, B. DADZIE, S. SCAFE, S (1985): *The Heart of the Race. Black Women's Lives in Britain.* Virago Press, London.

BUTTIMER, A and SEAMON, D (1980): *The Human Experience of Space and Place.* Croom Helm Ltd., London.

CAPRA, F and SPRETNAK, C (1984): *Green Politics. The Global Promise.* Hutchinson and Co. Ltd., London.

CHANDRA, B (1979): *Nationalism and Colonialism in Modern India.* Orient Longman Ltd., New Delhi.

DALPHINIS, M (1985): *Caribbean and African Languages. Social History, Language, Literature, and Education.* Karia Press, London

DENT, H.C. (1968): *The Education Act, 1944. Provisions, Regulations, Circulars, Later Acts.* Twelfth Edition. University of London Press Ltd.

ENGELS, F (1969): *The Condition of the Working Class in England.* Granada Publishing Ltd, London.

ENTWISTLE, H (1970): *Child-Centred Education.* (1977): *Class, Culture, and Education.* Methuen and Co., Ltd, London.

FRANCE, P and WILES, S (1984): *Working with young bilingual children.* ILEA, Centre for Urban Educational Studies, London.

FREIRE, P (1972): *Pedagogy of the Oppressed.* Penguin Books Ltd, London. (1972): *Cultural Action for Freedom.* Penguin Books Ltd, London.

FROMM, E (1979): *To Have or To Be?* Sphere Books Ltd, London.

FRYER, P (1984): *Staying Power. The History of Black People in Britain,* Pluto Press, London.

GANDHI, M.K (1982): *An Autobiography, or The Story of My Experiments With Truth.* Penguin Books, London.

GUNDARA, J. JONES, C. KIMBERLEY, K (1986): *Racism, Diversity, and Education.* Hodder and Stoughton Ltd, Kent.

HOBSBAWN, E.J (1968): *Industry and Empire.* Weidenfeld and Nicholson, London.

HOULTON, D and WILLEY, R (1983): *Supporting Children's Bilingualism. Some Policy issues for primary schools and local education authorities.* School Council Publications.

INNER LONDON EDUCATION AUTHORITY (1983): *Research and Statistics Report. 1983 Language Census.* (1985): *Research and Statistics Report. 1985 Language Census.*

JACKSON, B (1962): *Education and the Working Class.* Ark Paperbacks, Routledge and Kegan Paul, London.

KEDDIE, N (1973): *Tinker, Tailor ... The Myth of Cultural Deprivation.* Penguin Books, London.

LAPPING, B (1985): *End of Empire.* Granada Television Publications, Manchester.

LAWTON, D (1975): *Class, Culture, and the Curriculum.* Routledge and Kegan Paul, London.

LIDDLE, J and JOSHI, R (1986): *Daughters of Independence: Gender, Caste, and Class in India.* Zed Books Ltd, London.

MACKENZIE, J.M (1985): *Propaganda and Empire. The Manipulation of British public opinion 1880-1960.* Manchester University Press, Manchester.

MAZRUI, A.A (1986): *The Africans. A Triple Heritage.* BBC Publications, London.

MBITI, J.S (1969): *African Religions and Philosophy.* Heinemann Educational Books Ltd, London.

MILLER, J (1983): *Many Voices: Bilingualism, Culture, and Education.* Routledge and Kegan Paul, London.

MILNER, D (1983): *Children and Race ten years on.* Ward Lock Educational, London.

MUMFORD, L (1986): *The Future of Technics and Civilization.* Freedom Press, London.

ORZECHOWSKA, E (1984): *What it means to be a Bilingual Child in Britain Today.* Centre for Multicultural Education, University of London Institute of Education.

PATTANAYAK, D.P (1981): *Multilingualism and Mother-Tongue Education.* Oxford University Press, New Delhi.

PIAGET, J (1973): *The Child's Conception of the World.* Penguin Books, London.

PREISWERK, R and PERROT, D (1978): *Ethnocentrism and History. Africa, Asia, and Indian America in Western Textbooks.* NOK Publishers, USA.

RATHBONE, M and GRAHAM, N (1983): *Bilingual Nursery Assistants. Their use and training.* Schools Council Publications.

ROWBOTHAM, S. SEGAL, L. and WAINWRIGHT, H (1979): *Beyond The Fragments. Feminism and the Making of Socialism.* Merlin Press Ltd, London.

SAID, E.W (1978): *Orientalism.* Penguin Books, London.

SAMUEL, R (ed) (1981): *People's History and Socialist Theory.* Routledge and Kegan Paul, London.

SCHUMACHER, E.F (1974): *Small is Beautiful.* Sphere Books Ltd, London.

STEWART, J (1986): *The Making of the Primary School.* Open University Press, Milton Keynes.

STEDMAN JONES, G (1983): *Languages of Class. Studies in English Working-class History 1832-1982.* Cambridge University Press, Cambridge.

STONE, M (1981): *The Education of the Black Child in Britain.* Fontana Books, Oxford.

TEMPLE, R.K.G. (1986): *China: Land of Discovery and Invention.* Patrick Stephens Ltd, Wellingborough.

THOMPSON, E.P (1968): *The Making of the English Working Class.* Pelican Books, London.

VISTRAM, R (1986): *Ayahs, Lascars, and Princes. The Story of Indians in Britain 1700-1947.* Pluto Press, London.

WARD, C(1979): *The Child in the City.* Penguin Books, London.

WOLF, E.R (1982): *Europe and The People Without History.* University of California Press Ltd, Berkeley.